HAWAII

PHOENIX
IS.

TOKELAUS

MARQUESAS

SAMOA

TUAMOTUS

COOKS

TAHITI

TONGA

AUSTRALS

Easter'

The Pacific Area

ANCIENT VOYAGERS IN POLYNESIA

Ancient Voyagers in Polynesia

by

ANDREW SHARP

UNIVERSITY OF CALIFORNIA PRESS

BERKELEY AND LOS ANGELES

1964

Published in the United States of America by
University of California Press
Berkeley and Los Angeles, California

Published in New Zealand by
Paul's Book Arcade, Auckland and Hamilton

PRINTED IN AUSTRALIA

33,438

PREFACE

It is now over six years since my previous book *Ancient Voyagers in the Pacific* was first published by the Polynesian Society, and over five years since it was reprinted by Penguin Books in their Pelican series. During these years I have gathered upwards of a hundred published notices of the book, have had a dozen protracted and interesting exchanges of letters with experts of various sorts, and have been involved in 2,191 oral discussions of the book's themes. I have yet to hear of a fact or read an argument which impugns the basic contentions of the former book, but the present book, while based on the previous one, offers some advances on my previous views. The change of title to *Ancient Voyagers in Polynesia* indicates that Polynesia occupies the foreground, as indeed it did in the book's predecessor, but I have still attempted to view the Polynesian themes in relation to early oceanic voyaging elsewhere. There is sufficient new material in *Ancient Voyagers in Polynesia* to justify the claim that it is in considerable degree a new book.

I am indebted to the Polynesian Society for having provided me with a first forum for a number of my views in its memoir series and journal.

'Western Polynesia' in the present book means the Tonga-Samoa-Ellice-Tokelau area, and 'Eastern Polynesia' the Cook-Tahiti-Tuamotu-Mangareva-Marquesas-Easter Island area.

Andrew Sharp.

CONTENTS

CONTENTS

LIST OF ILLUSTRATIONS

PLATES

LIST OF ILLUSTRATIONS

FIGURES

MAPS

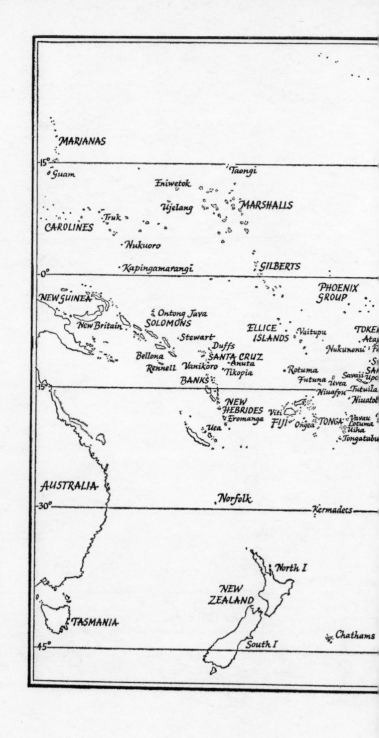

HAWAII
Oahu
Hawaii

15°

Palmyra
Washington
Fanning
Christmas
Jarvis

0°

Malden
Starbuck

LAUS
kaofo
vains
Manua

NORTHERN COOKS
Rakahanga Tongareva
Pukapuka Manihiki
Nassau

Nuku Hiva MARQUESAS
Ua Pou Hiva Oa

utabu
Viue

Takaroa

Borabora
Raiatea Tahiti
Palmerston
Aitutaki
Mehetia
Amaa Hao
Atiu Mauke
SOUTHERN
COOKS Rarotonga
Mangaia
Mitiaro

Pukapuka
TUAMOTUS

15°

Rurutu
Rimatara Tubuai
Raivavae
AUSTRALS

Mangareva
Pitcairn

Rapa

30°

The Pacific Islands

Scale of Miles

At 45° 400 300 200 100 0 100 200 300 400 At 45°
At 30° At 30°
At 15° At 15°
At 0° At 0°

45°

CHAPTER ONE

A WORLD PERSPECTIVE

EVER since European explorers found people with brown skins, speaking dialects of the same language, on all the inhabited islands in the area since known as Polynesia, the problems associated with early Polynesian voyaging and settlement have engaged men's minds. Some of the Polynesian islands—Hawaii, New Zealand, Easter Island—are 1,000 to 1,800 miles from the nearest other inhabited land. It will be our task in this book to discuss the interesting issues arising from the arrival of the Polynesians, their dispersal throughout their far-flung islands, and the manner of their voyaging.

Over the past eighty years most people have imagined that the farther islands of Polynesia were discovered by prehistoric navigators who sailed back to their home islands and organized colonizing expeditions to their discoveries. Yet the key to the truth about the manner of the Polynesian dispersal was left by the greatest of Pacific explorers before death suddenly claimed him.

Captain James Cook quitted the shores of New Zealand for the last time on 25 February 1777,[1] and sailed east. After he had run east and then north-east for five weeks, land was sighted. This was the island of Mangaia in the Southern Cook Group. From Mangaia Cook's two ships sailed on, and 140 miles to the north, Atiu came into view. Cook was the first European explorer to make contact with these islands.

The people of Atiu proved friendly, and some interesting information was exchanged through Omai, Cook's Tahitian interpreter. Omai was surprised to find on Atiu three of his countrymen from Tahiti, over 600 miles to the north-east. They were the survivors of a canoe which had been blown away in a sudden gale while passing from Tahiti to Raiatea, an important island about 100 miles west of Tahiti. After many days they came to Atiu. This had happened long before, and in the meantime the Tahitians had settled happily in their new home.

By 1777 Cook had traversed the Pacific several times. He now had first-hand evidence of the accidental one-way voyage of the Tahitians to Atiu. He was also familiar with Charles de Brosses's accounts of Pacific voyages, which told the story of a more significant involuntary migration. In 1696 a large canoe made an accidental journey from the Caroline Islands in the North Pacific to the Philippines, having been lost at sea in a storm while passing between two local islands. After seventy days it arrived on the island of Samar, 1,000 miles away, with a number of men, women, children and babies, none of whom had any idea where they were.[2]

Cook therefore knew enough to give a tentative explanation of the peopling of the detached islands of the world. In his journal account of the voyage of the Tahitians to Atiu, he wrote that this incident 'will serve to explain, better than the thousand conjectures of speculative reasoners, how the detached parts of the earth, and, in particular, how the South Seas, may have been peopled; particularly those that lie remote from any inhabited continent, or from each other'.

Later evidence, reviewed in Chapter Four, indicates that, as well as people who were blown away in storms, voluntary exiles and exiles driven out to sea arrived on other islands by one-way voyages in which deliberate navigation to those islands played no part. The term 'one-way settlement' is a convenient one for migration by one-way voyages arising either from storms or exile.

Cook did not limit his hypothesis to prehistoric Polynesian settlement, but suggested that it applied also to other detached parts of the world. It is desirable, therefore, to view the voyages

Original by Conrad Martens, artist on FitzRoy's voyage in the *Beagle*. Sailing canoes of this type were in danger of being overset by a sudden gust on the lee side when sailing close to the wind, particularly in areas of variable winds. Furthermore, if narrow enough in the beam to have a good resistance to leeway when tacking, their carrying capacity on long settlement voyages was correspondingly limited.

of the Polynesians in relation to the whole pageant of man's going down to the sea in ships. Two centuries of navigation by the highly sophisticated system of latitude and longitude, which took 5,000 years to evolve, have made us forget the romance and difficulties of early voyaging without modern aids.

Man originated as a land animal and presumably graduated through river craft to coastal vessels. The early off-shore voyages of the Old World were in land-locked seas to extended coasts. Crude methods of navigation by the sun, stars, and wind directions were good enough for voyages of no great distance between extended coasts, because a landfall somewhere or other was assured, even if the precise destination were missed. The voyagers could thus maintain a broad course by bearings in relation to the east-west paths of the stars and sun and their rising and setting points, and the north bearing of the Pole Star. When they came in sight of the coast, which they could not miss, they could pick their way along it. The early Phoenicians, Greeks, Romans, and Scandinavians travelled in this manner across the Mediterranean, the Black Sea, the Baltic and the North Sea. The Arabs and Indians sailed across the Arabian Gulf, where they were aided by the monsoons which blow steadily in one direction at one part of the year and in the reverse direction at the other. Steady winds have an advantage as a navigation aid—they continue to blow when the sun and stars are obscured.

The islands within the land-locked seas and gulfs, and the chains of islands within easy reach of the continents and one another, such as the West Indian and East Indian islands, Formosa, and Japan, did not make any great demand on navigation.

Ocean islands which were more than 300 miles from the continents or from one another were in an entirely different class. There was no way of finding they existed by crossing between coasts as in the land-locked seas and gulfs. The idea of systematic exploration involves the presumption that explorers were prepared to go twice as far as any island they happened to find,

B

and to do so many times without success, for an explorer cannot hope to find new land more than very occasionally, if at all. Above all, unless one can fix the position of the island one finds, and plot a course from it and back to it again, two-way contact is not established. If a voyager were blown to an ocean island by a storm, he had still less chance of noting his course to it and getting home again.

The first step toward the development of instrumental navigation on long voyages out of sight of land was made with the use of crude compasses to keep a bearing on the north when the skies were obscured. These enabled navigators to maintain their directions independently of the heavenly bodies and the directions of wind and sea, making them aware of changes of wind even when the stars were covered with cloud. Compasses, however, did not give any assurance of a landfall on a small objective or a distant ocean island, since compass bearings give no clue to lateral displacements with currents and winds.

The next great advance was the application of the principle of the quadrant as a means of judging the altitude above the horizon of the Pole Star and the sun, and of determining latitude therefrom. The Pole Star was, however, not a great deal of use for this purpose, because, during most of the time that it is visible, the horizon is indistinct. The sun has the advantage over the stars that, when it is visible at high noon, the horizon is usually visible too. Land-bound astronomers achieved the great revolution of determining latitude from the sun when they found that, provided the date is kept as accurately as possible on a voyage, changes in the altitude of the sun above the horizon at high noon as it moves toward the northern or southern solstice can be allowed for, and latitude determined by adding or subtracting the appropriate compensation.

The Portuguese and Spaniards used astrolabes to cross the oceans. Since their use required some knowledge of arithmetic, and of the sun's movements in relation to the calendar, the profession of pilot came into existence. Provided the navigator knew that he was east or west of his objective when he started, he could pick up ocean islands by keeping in the latitude in which they had previously been found. On courses with a predominant northing or southing component, however, the problem of longitude still remained, for quadrants give no clue to lateral displacements on such courses. This problem was not solved satisfactorily until the eighteenth century, when lunar observations and finally chronometers enabled navigators to fix their positions from the intersections of parallels of latitude and meridians of longitude.

In crossing the Atlantic and Indian Oceans, the Portuguese and Spaniards happened on a number of ocean islands; others were discovered by ships blown to them in storms.[3] The Atlantic coasts of Spain, Portugal, and Africa were a great deal more suitable than islands were as bases for the prehistoric discovery of the Atlantic islands and their subsequent colonization, for the voyagers could regain the coast somewhere or other if, after making their discoveries, they tried to get back home. They would still have had to find the discoveries again if they wanted to colonize them. If prehistoric navigators attempted such feats of deliberate exploration followed by colonization, apparently none succeeded, as the following notes will show.

The Atlantic islands of Madeira are particularly suited to human settlement. They lie only 330 miles from the coast of Africa, and 530 miles from Lisbon, which have been areas of maritime enterprise since the dawn of history. When they were discovered in 1418 by a Portuguese ship which was blown to them in a storm, they were uninhabited. Today their population is a quarter of a million or more.

The Azores, a group of sunny and attractive islands about 800 miles west of Portugal, were unsettled until Europeans came upon them in the fifteenth century.

The Cape Verde Islands lie about 400 miles off the coast of Africa. When discovered by a Portuguese ship in 1456, they were uninhabited. The detached Atlantic islands of Bermuda, St Helena, Ascension, and Tristan da Cunha were also all uninhabited when discovered in comparatively late times.

Mauritius, Reunion, and the Chagos Archipelago, in the Indian Ocean, were uninhabited when the Portuguese found them. They are well populated today.

To complete the world-wide picture of the discovery of distant ocean islands, Juan Fernandez, the Falklands, and numbers of others were uninhabited when the Europeans encountered them.

On the other hand, settlements compatible with a theory of one-way voyaging were found on Madagascar, several hundred miles off the African coast. This island was inhabited by people with linguistic and cultural affinities with the Indonesians far to the east across the Indian Ocean. These affinities can be explained by the view that Madagascar was settled by one-way voyagers coming directly from the East Indies to Madagascar. The prevailing winds and currents from the East Indies to Madagascar are among the most constant in the world. Madagascar is a big island which might be expected to lie in the path of occasional voyagers from the East Indies, although none established themselves upon the smaller intervening islands in the Indian Ocean. The presence of East Indian cultivated plants in Madagascar is consistent with this view, since exiles might have set out with them, or voyagers endeavouring to take them to other islands in the East Indies might have been blown away. Since Africa is bigger than Madagascar, and not a great deal farther from the East Indies, it is probable that Indonesians were occasionally borne on one-way voyages to Africa itself.

We find, then, that prehistoric peopling of the farther ocean islands of the world was confined to a few islands in the Indian Ocean and numbers of islands in the Pacific. These islands lie on either side of the chain of islands stretching from Sumatra to Formosa, forming an archipelago favourable to the development of local voyaging and with oceans dotted with islands on either side. These geographical conditions were well suited to the settlement of Madagascar and the Pacific Islands by one-way migrants from the islands off the south coast of Asia.

The Polynesian and Viking voyages have often been compared, but the resemblance between the areas in which they were made is not as close as the comparisons suggest.

It is a matter of history that Scandinavians were crossing the North Sea to the north of Scotland and Ireland somewhere round the eighth century A.D. These voyages were indeed spectacular, but they were between extended coasts over distances of several hundred miles.

The Icelandic saga of the arrival of the Norse says that Irishmen were the first to reach Iceland, a large island some 300 miles north of the British Isles.[4] The people of Iceland are of mixed Celtic and Scandinavian origin. Suggestions have been made that the Scandinavians discovered Iceland by deliberate exploration. Heaven forbid that it should be concluded that the Irish got there by accident, while the Scandinavian cousins of the Anglo-Saxons showed greater ingenuity! Perhaps the Scandinavians came on Iceland in the course of their voyages across the North Sea to the British Isles.

Going a little farther afield to Greenland, that Scandinavian settlements existed there in early times is proved by the archaeological evidence of burials and ruins.[5] There is no difficulty in believing that Greenland was colonized by two-way contact following on accidental discovery from Iceland, for the distance separating the two islands is under 200 miles at the nearest point, and there is an extended coast on either side of the waters dividing them. Investigation of the burials in modern times appears to suggest that malnutrition had something to do with the cessation of Scandinavian settlement.

What, then, of the reputed Viking visits to America? It is not impossible that Scandinavian voyagers reached the shores of America and then got home again, since America, Greenland, Iceland and Europe present wide targets for primitive navigators and the winds and currents are not unfavourable. The fact remains, however, that the evidence is remarkably thin. Those who believe—on the evidence of Scandinavian sagas written several centuries after the events they relate, and including typical folk-lore of fairy-like beings in far lands—that Bjarni, Leif Ericsson and others went to America and back, are entitled to do so if they can. Others may prefer to suspect that Vinland, the Land of Perpetual Summer, was placed by the story-tellers in the western ocean because there was nowhere else to put it, like the Islands of the Blest of the ancients, and the Avalon and Saint Brendan's Island of the Celts. The tales of early Viking visits to America have been supposed to be supported by similar tales from Polynesia and vice versa, but on examination this mutual support collapses. If indubitable relics of prehistoric Scandinavian occupation in North America are ever forthcoming, they may not prove anything more than that one-way voyagers occasionally reached America.

Some students of prehistory—in their determination not to consider the possibility of long, one-way voyages by sea—have shown a preference for land bridges or chains of islands as routes for early human migration into the Americas and Australia.

The Behring Strait area may indeed have been the primary route of entry into North America. It is not impossible, however, that later one-way migrants were borne to North America by the Japan Current and the westerlies of higher latitudes. In historical times there have been a number of instances where Japanese fishing vessels have been driven to America in this way.

When Matthew Flinders sailed along the north coast of Australia's Northern Territory in the early nineteenth century, he met Malays in canoes from the Celebes area of the East Indies.[6] They told him that their attention had been attracted to Australia by an accidental voyage to the north coast of some compatriots and their successful return. This evidence shows that voyages from the Timor area could and did occur by accident with the north-west monsoon. In the instance mentioned, the migrants got back to the East Indies. This incident led to annual visits to gather trepang for the Chinese trade. The navigators did not navigate by the stars, but used a Dutch compass. In making these visits they had the advantage of the north-west monsoon of the summer months on the outward leg, and the south-east trade wind on the return leg, with wide targets of islands and coast on both legs. Their use of the Dutch compass falls short of supporting a theory that there was systematic two-way contact between the East Indies and the north coast of Australia in ancient times.

In view of this evidence, it seems unnecessary to assume that all the early migrants to Australia came by way of an early land bridge corresponding to the chains of islands between New Guinea and Australia. One or more voyages on crude craft with the north-west monsoon to the Northern Territory area of Australia may have occurred.

The inclusion of women on such voyages would no doubt have been rare. The case of Annika Lotte and her sister, however, may be evidence in support of the possibility.[7] Annika was one of ten Indonesian men and women who survived a 400-mile, five-week accidental voyage across the Timor Sea to the Northern Territory. She ran off into the bush in terror, and for four weeks lived on local vegetation. Eventually she was found and reunited to her sister, another survivor of this voyage.

A. Capell, an Australian linguist, in a recent summary, says that the linguistic evidence points to a widespread affinity among the aboriginal speeches apart from Tasmanian, the relationship of which is doubtful.[8] There is cultural evidence, and possibly biological evidence also, of continuing infiltrations into the northern areas of Australia, particularly those near and south of Cape York Peninsula.[9] What appears to be needed, therefore, is a theory of settlement by a few people whose descendants spread through the continent in comparative isolation, followed by further infiltrations into the northern areas. One-way migration across the Timor Sea may have accounted for the arrival of some of the settlers.

The possibility of later Polynesian one-way voyages to the east coast of Australia can by no means be ruled out. No doubt any Polynesians who gained a foothold there would in due course have been absorbed.

Continuing our comparative survey of early voyaging, we come to the Micronesian groups in the North Pacific. There is much evidence from European explorers about voyages within the Western Caroline archipelago. All the islands can be reached without covering gaps of more than 170 miles, but direct passages of up to 360 miles, by-passing intervening islands, were made.[10] The Caroline sea-going canoes were built with single outriggers which were always kept on the windward side. These canoes were adequate for the Caroline sailing season when the prevailing trade wind was steady from the east. The central islands of the archipelago were the cradle of the maritime arts, no doubt because they were near one another, and the screens of islands round them gave the voyagers defence in depth in their sea passages.

When the author of the present book was writing its predecessor, *Ancient Voyagers in the Pacific*, Thomas Gladwin, an American ethnologist, was independently writing of his observations in the Truk area of the Western Carolines, where local voyagers still sail their outrigger canoes without precision instruments.[11] Gladwin came to the same conclusions as did the present author in his own book: namely, that the inherent defect in such navigation without instruments on the open sea was that it was fundamentally a dead reckoning system dependent on calculating and allowing for set with currents and drift with winds, and that when errors or failures in dead reckoning occurred, the voyagers were powerless to detect or correct them. Gladwin's views were later published in the *American Anthropologist*.

In the late nineteenth and early twentieth centuries, a succession of European visitors to Micronesia questioned various islanders about their geographical knowledge and the extent of their voyaging.[12] They found that the islanders knew the names of islands at a distance, and sometimes had traditions of deliberate visits to them. These inquirers, from Kubary to the ethnologists of the German South Sea Expedition in the early twentieth century, assumed that these traditions were valid evidence of former deliberate two-way contacts. All that this indirect oral evidence proved, however, was that the Micronesians of the late nineteenth and early twentieth centuries had some knowledge of the geography of the Pacific; it threw no light on how that knowledge was gained, whether from accidental voyages to distant islands and successful returns, or from information brought by one-way voyagers from those islands, or from knowledge imparted by European visitors or islanders who had sailed in European ships. Least of all did the late evidence gleaned by European visitors to Micronesia apply to the circumstances attending the prehistoric discovery and settlement of its manifold islands at times when those islands were uninhabited and unknown.

The Marshalls were a Micronesian group with interesting local features. When the Russian explorer O. von Kotzebue visited this group early in the nineteenth century, a chief described how he sailed between the eastern and western sectors of the group, over a distance of a hundred odd miles. The two sectors offered a wide screen to voyagers on both legs. Furthermore, there are 867 reefs in the group, and reefs were like signposts to navigators in shallow-draught vessels. It is no wonder there were reports in later days of records, made by means of shells and strings, of the locations of islands and the swing and variation of local currents. Yet neither on these shell-and-string charts, nor in a map of the Marshalls which Kotzebue made from the information given him by Marshallese voyagers, was there any sign of Ujelang, Eniwetok and Taongi, three detached atolls of the group. Furthermore the only knowledge the informants had of the Gilberts, several hundred miles to the south, was from accidental voyagers.[13]

When Captain Hudson and Horatio Hale, of the United States Exploring Expedition of 1838-1842, visited the Gilbert and Ellice Islands in 1841, these groups were still little known. The Americans found by systematic inquiry[14] that the Gilbertese voyaged only between the central islands of the group, and that contact even within these islands was limited and discontinuous. Thus neither of two Europeans who had been living for several years in the Gilberts knew that the other was there. The southern Ellice Islanders showed no sign of knowing the Gilberts or other islands to the north. The Gilbert and Ellice Islands form a thin chain across the prevailing winds and currents, making voyaging so hazardous that the Gilbertese had a customary law that when some of their people were swept away in storms, their property was divided after a certain time.[15] Nor were storms the only danger. A sailing schooner once took six weeks to pass between two Gilbertese islands thirty-five miles apart, another took three weeks for a passage of 270 miles.[16] These difficulties occurred, not as the result of unfavourable winds, but in the season when the winds were fitful and the current became the master. The worst situation for any sailing vessel is to be caught by a current in unknown waters without a wind.

Kotzebue's, Hudson's and Hale's evidence of the discontinuous nature of contact between and within the Marshalls, Gilberts, and Ellice Islands, coupled with the local circumstances of current and wind that have been considered in this section, make it probable that these groups formed a sort of no-man's-land between the main Micronesian and Polynesian areas, and got one-way migrants from both. Hudson and Hale thought that some of the inhabitants of the Gilbert and Ellice Islands resembled the people of the Carolines in appearance and culture, and that others were like the Samoans.

Having seen the challenging and fruitful nature of Cook's hypothesis when applied to the detached parts of the world outside Polynesia, we now return to Atiu in the Cook Group in 1777. It had taken Cook five weeks to get from New Zealand to the Cooks, and he was still 600 miles from Tahiti. Rather than fight against the wind and current from the east, he decided to run west to the Tonga Group, a distance of about 1,000 miles. These facts do not support the conventional view that prehistoric navigators from Tahiti and Rarotonga, having discovered New Zealand, established two-way contact between their discovery and their home islands.

In the Tonga Group Cook and his men spent five pleasant months. He and his associate, William Anderson, who was officially in charge of natural history observations, as well as being ship's surgeon, took advantage of the long stay to find out from the Tongans the state of their geographical knowledge.

At that time the Tongans ranged far and wide over the adjacent islands. To the north-east their trips extended to the Samoa Group. To the west of the Tongans lived the formidable Fijians, whom the more daring Tongan chiefs occasionally visited; Cook met some Fijian visitors to Tonga. On these journeys, each of 360 miles, the longest gaps are of 180 miles from Vavau to Niuatobutabu on the way to Samoa, and of 220 miles from Tonga to Ongea, on the way to Viti, the main island of the Fiji Group.

The Tongans gave Cook a list of 156 islands known to them. Anderson, says Cook, wrote every one of them down. Most of the names in this list can be identified. They account for the great majority of the manifold islands of Tonga, and all the main islands of Samoa. Viti appears in the spelling 'Feejee', from which the group derives its name. Viti is on the farther side of the Fiji Group from Tonga, and it is not surprising that some of the islands in between are identifiable. 'Toggelao', which may well be the Tokelau Group, some 300 miles north of Samoa, is in the list. Whether the Tongans themselves visited the Tokelaus is an open question, since there are records of accidental voyages from the Tokelaus to islands in the Tonga area in later times,[17] and it is possible that the Tongans of Cook's day knew of the group from earlier incidents of this nature. The list contains no sign of the Cooks or Tahitian islands to the east.

The information Cook gleaned about Western Polynesian voyages is supplemented by that given to W. Mariner and P. Dillon,[18] two later Europeans who knew the western area in the early nineteenth century, and by George Turner,[19] an early missionary in Samoa. Mariner and Dillon said that the Tongans occasionally exchanged visits with the people of Rotuma, a largish high island 300 miles to the north-west of the archipelago formed by the Fiji and Tonga Groups.

Dillon's evidence also shows that the Rotumans were in contact with the southern islands of the Ellice Group as far as Vaitupu, the name of which also appears in Cook's list of islands known to the Tongans. The nearest of the Ellice Islands to Rotuma is 200 miles away.

Dillon said that the Fijians and Samoans visited Tonga only as passengers in Tongan canoes, and George Turner said that the Samoans did not go outside their own islands. The Tongans were thus the main voyagers in the Fiji-Tonga-Samoa area, no doubt because of their central position in relation to the other groups. Since the Tongans were in touch with Rotuma, and the Rotumans with the southern Ellice Islands, it is probable that the Tongans occasionally paid visits to the latter islands by way of Rotuma. It is interesting to note that when Hudson and Hale visited the southern Ellice Islands in 1841, the islanders described bananas as fruit of Rotuma.[20]

There is thus firm evidence of two-way contacts in early

historical times between Tonga, Fiji, Samoa, Rotuma, and the
Ellice Islands.

On the other hand, Dillon found evidence indicating that
the Tongans in early historical times did not know of islands
to the west of Rotuma. He wrote: 'Thubow (chief of Tonga)
inquired of me this morning at breakfast where Mannicolo lay,
for that, in all of the voyages of the Tonga people among the
islands, they had never heard of the Mannicolos. I informed
him that it was close to Tikopia, an island of which he also
expressed his ignorance.' Tikopia and Vanikoro (Dillon's
'Mannicolos') lie 500 and 600 miles beyond Rotuma to the west.
Although Tubou did not know of these islands, lost canoes of
Tongan raiders may have encountered them, for Dillon found
that the Tikopians had a tradition of an attack by Tongans.

From Tonga Cook sailed back east to Tahiti, taking about
three weeks. During this time squalls sometimes blew from the
north and west. In Tahiti Cook was on familiar ground. He
was not the first European to visit Tahiti, which was discovered
by the Englishman S. Wallis in 1767, and visited by the French-
man L. A. de Bougainville in 1768. But from 1769, until he left
Tahiti finally in 1777, after the visit we are discussing, Cook
spent over a year in the Tahitian islands in all.

During the five months which Cook's company spent there
on this last visit before going north, Anderson made some more
fact-finding inquiries. He interviewed the Tahitian voyagers,
who told him that the canoemen of Anaa and the other nearer
islands of the Tuamotu Group, 170 to 230 miles east of the
Tahitian islands, exchanged visits with them. The Tahitians
also appeared to know of other islands at a distance without
ever having visited them, and Anderson concluded that this
knowledge was derived from accidental voyagers who had come
from these islands to the Tahitian islands. His view was that
the Tahitian voyages were confined to the Tahitian islands
and the nearer Tuamotus.

In reaching these views, Anderson was going against Cook's

own surmises at the time of his first visit to Tahiti in 1769.[21] There Cook had met Tupaea, a chief of the Tahitian island of Raiatea, who had been defeated and driven to Tahiti. Tupaea claimed a considerable knowledge of the surrounding islands, and Cook and his associates took him with them as guide and interpreter. He died in Batavia later in the voyage. Tupaea with his own hands, said Cook, drew a chart showing seventy-four islands known to the Tahitians. Cook listed the names of these in his journal, together with their compass directions from Tahiti. He marked those which Tupaea claimed he had visited. At that time Cook thought that the Tahitians were in contact with islands at considerable distances from Tahiti. It was highly significant, therefore, when he included in his journal of the third voyage Anderson's refutation of the earlier surmises concerning Tahitian deliberate long two-way voyaging made by Cook and his associates and by Bougainville.

Anderson said that it was improbable that Tupaea had visited a certain island 'Oheteroa' before coming to it with Cook in the *Endeavour* in 1769, despite Tupaea's claim to have visited it previously. 'Oheteroa' was in fact Rurutu, some 320 miles south of the Tahitian islands, although this name was not known until long after Anderson and Cook were dead.[22] In the list of islands Tupaea gave Cook, Rurutu and 'Oheteroa' are shown as separate islands. Another island which Tupaea thought was in the same quarter and claimed to have visited was named 'Mannua'. Evidence will be given in Chapter Five for the view that the names 'Oheteroa' and 'Mannua' betokened traditional memories of Viti in the Fiji Group and Manua in the Samoa Group, brought from Western Polynesia to Eastern Polynesia by one-way migrants.

Anderson also discounted Bougainville's conjectures that the Tahitians made voyages of 900 miles, during which they lost sight of land for lengthy periods and sailed by the sun and stars.[23] Bougainville had been told by a Tahitian informant that voyages lasting fifteen days were sometimes made. These statements, however, are not positive assertions that ocean voyages of such a length were made. Bougainville himself had just come through the Tuamotu Group stretching over a distance of more than 700 miles, and had heard from his informant of the western sector of the Tahitian islands. When, therefore, Anderson concluded that the Tahitians went no farther afield than the nearer Tuamotus, and opposed Bougainville's opinion, the issue was really one of how far the Tahitians voyaged in the Tuamotu Group.

Andia y Varela, the captain of one of the ships of a Spanish expedition to Tahiti in 1772-1775, was told by the Tahitians that they visited the western sector of the Tahitian islands, about 100 miles to the west of Tahiti, and Andia's colleagues were told of visits to the nearer Tuamotus.[24] The Spaniards did not hear of any longer voyages, although they questioned the Tahitians closely concerning their geographical knowledge.

It is evident that Cook, far from being an authority who supports the belief in Polynesian voyaging to and from distant islands, is decidedly the opposite. On his third voyage, after having traversed the Pacific several times, he quotes Anderson in indirect refutation of his own earlier surmises about such voyages, cites evidence that accidental voyages conveyed people and knowledge between distant islands, and suggests that the dispersal of man in general, and of the Polynesians in particular, was brought about by similar voyages.

It cannot be said that Cook put forward this explanation as a final conclusion. He and Anderson did not have sufficient geographical knowledge to eliminate the possibility that there were undiscovered islands which might have formed links between the discovered ones. Nor did Cook mention the possibility that voluntary and forced exile led to the discovery and settlement of distant islands by one-way migrants. He was, however, perceptive enough to put forward something approaching a realistic hypothesis of the prehistoric settlement of the detached islands of the world.

Within a short time of giving their mature thoughts in a few pregnant paragraphs here and there in the journal of the third voyage, Cook and Anderson were both dead.

In sum, positive evidence of the range of Polynesian cruising in the accounts of early European contacts with Polynesia does not support the view that two-way voyages over long distances were made at that time. The only islands between which there are firm records of deliberate two-way contact over gaps of more than 100 miles without intervening islands were Rarotonga and Atiu (116 miles), the Tahitian islands and the Tuamotu Group (170 to 230 miles), Rotuma and the Ellice Islands (200 miles), Tonga and Fiji (220 miles), the Fiji-Tonga area and Rotuma (300 odd miles), and Tonga and Samoa (180 miles to Niuatobutabu and Tafahi and 170 miles thence to Savaii, or 360 miles direct).

The Polynesians, like the Western Caroline Islanders, indeed deserve their reputation as outstanding voyagers. In making visits to islands several hundred miles away without instruments, they were heroes of the sea whose like may never be seen again.

TONGAN SAILING SHIP

Original by John Webber, artist on Cook's third voyage.

CHAPTER TWO

HOW DID THE POLYNESIANS
NAVIGATE?

IT is essential to have clear views on the issues involved in the prehistoric discovery of distant ocean islands. A little thought will show that all the distant ocean islands in the world must have been encountered in the first place by accident, and not by deliberate navigation to those islands. Navigation implies that the existence and location of one's objective is known, and a course set for it. Unless and until the objective has been discovered, navigation is not an issue. Nor does the mere discovery of new land mean that deliberate navigation from it occurred thereafter. Navigation comes into the picture only when one imagines the discoverers of distant ocean islands or their descendants using knowledge gained on a voyage of discovery as a means of setting a deliberate course to their home islands. One object of the present chapter is to show that, in the case of New Zealand, Hawaii, and the other detached Polynesian islands, the prehistoric discoverers had no way of gaining the knowledge necessary for navigation back to their home islands. It will follow that the settlement of these detached islands was contemporaneous with their discovery. The other object of the chapter is to review the methods of navigation used by the Polynesians on their authenticated voyages at the time of early European contact.

Although deliberate navigation did not enter into the discovery of the detached islands of Polynesia, deliberate exploration could have been a factor. People who set out in the hope of finding new land were certainly explorers, though not deliberate navigators to any land they found. People who were blown away while on voyages to local islands, moreover, could

c

in many cases have searched for land in order to get themselves out of their predicament, and so have made discoveries by exploration. No more unfortunate term than 'drift voyages' could be applied to these processes of discovery accompanied by settlement.

People who say that there must have been some deliberate navigation to the detached islands of Polynesia in order to account for their prehistoric settlement overlook the fact that all these far-flung islands were encountered accidentally in the first place. Nothing is added by arguing that navigation entered into the process.

It will be convenient first to consider the evidence of Poly-nesian navigation at the time of European contact. The Tongans, as we have seen in Chapter One, were in touch with Fiji, Samoa, and Rotuma. They told Cook that they sailed by the sun and stars, and that when these heavenly guides were obscured, they judged their courses in relation to the direction of the wind and surface seas. The Tahitians told Cook and Andia y Varela, the Spanish captain who visited Tahiti at about the same time as Cook, that they used these same methods on their voyages within the Tahitian islands and to the nearer Tuamotus. The direction of the wind and seas was the only guide when the sky became obscured. If at such a time the wind changed, the Tongans told Cook that their navigators were 'bewildered, fre-quently miss their intended port and are never heard of more'.[1]

An ingenious way of recording the directions of journeys when they had been determined by experience was to pick out two landmarks on the starting point which were in line with the desired course. The voyagers could start off in the afternoon, lining up the landmarks with their craft until they faded from sight, and then take up the course by bearings on stars, thereby reducing their dependence on the sun, which is a poor guide. John Williams was told of the use of this method on voyages from Atiu to Rarotonga, 116 miles south.[2] When Beechey visited the Tuamotus in 1824, he heard from some voyagers of Anaa that when leaving for the Tahitian island of Mehetia, 170 miles to the west, they set their direction by landmarks on Anaa in the same way.[3]

These methods of navigation without instruments show a remarkable adaptation to the environment in which the voyagers found themselves. We shall see in the next section of the present chapter the severe limitations inherent in astral navigation without instruments even when the skies were clear. The voyagers supplemented their astral navigation by using the wind direction and the run of the seas as a sort of crude compass needle. Their methods, of course, differed radically from those of a modern navigator. Because overstatements of Polynesian long navigation have obscured the issues, the ancient voyagers are not given due credit for their ingenuity and daring in establishing contact with islands several hundred miles away.

We come now to the facts of physical geography which refute the view that prehistoric Polynesians, having discovered distant islands, sailed back to their home islands by deliberate navigation and mounted colonizing expeditions to the discoveries.

First, oceanography. As the earth rotates on its axis from west to east, the land masses and islands tend to move faster than the seas, setting up complex and variable ocean currents. These processes have been going on since long before man entered the Pacific. But no navigator, whether prehistoric Polynesian or modern European, has ever seen a Pacific current operate on his vessel on the open sea, for the simple reason that the vessel and the body of water surrounding it move imperceptibly together. The way in which Europeans when out of sight of land gained a broad knowledge of the set of the Pacific currents was by many comparisons of hypothetical dead reckoning positions with the true positions as determined by precision instruments over two centuries of Pacific exploration. These facts of oceanography are too often overlooked by theorists of Polynesian navigation over long distances.

Errors in the judgment of bearings resulting from miscalculations of drift with winds are another hazard on long ocean voyages in sailing craft.

Coming now to astronomy. As the earth rotates on its axis, the stars and sun appear to pass from east to west. As they do so they give navigators without instruments no guide to relative longitudes. There are no stable points of reference in the westing paths of the stars and sun whereby longitudinal deviations to the west or east on long northing and southing courses as the result of transverse currents or miscalculations of drift with winds could be detected and corrected in the days before instruments. Yet it is between islands situated at great distances in northing and southing directions from each other that the feats of prehistoric Polynesian navigation as an accompaniment of colonization are supposed to have occurred: namely the Gilberts-Tahiti, the Gilberts-Samoa, Tahiti-Hawaii, Tahiti-Rarotonga, Rarotonga-New Zealand, Tahiti-New Zealand, the Southern Cooks-Northern Cooks, the Marquesas-Hawaii, the Marquesas-Mangareva, the Marquesas-Easter Island.

The rest of this section will consider the inherent limitations on navigation without instruments which refute the various theories of prehistoric Polynesian navigation as an accompaniment to the settlement of distant islands.

A well-established method of primitive navigation on short journeys is to sail toward a point marked by a succession of rising or setting stars known from previous experience to be in line with the desired objective. Many theorists, therefore, have pictured the Polynesians as sailing to distant objectives by aiming towards horizon stars which, from previous exploratory probes, were known to be in the appropriate direction. This method of navigation, however, gives no clue to longitudinal displacement as the result of currents and miscalculations of drift with winds. It is practicable, therefore, only on short journeys where the effects of set with currents and drift with winds can be judged with sufficient accuracy to allow of the sighting of the objective before the voyagers are displaced off course and carried past the objective without seeing it. All that the horizon stars can do is to give a crude bearing at the time

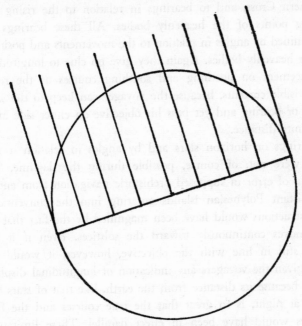

FIG. 1. Courses on Horizon Stars

A course toward a point on the horizon marked by successive rising stars gives no clue to lateral displacement because each horizon star is seen as a horizon star by every observer on a great circle extending round the earth.

the voyagers start their journey. Horizon stars give no indication of longitudinal displacement because each horizon star, as it rises or sets, is billions of miles away, whereas the diameter of the earth is less than 8,000 miles. The true course and all the possible false courses arising from longitudinal displacement all the way round the world, therefore, are parallel and undifferentiable. For this reason, even on short journeys, courses by bearings on horizon stars are risky.

The defect applying to the use of horizon stars applies also to bearings in relation to the east-west paths of the sun and stars and the north-south lines given by the Pole Star and the Southern Cross, and to bearings in relation to the rising and setting points of the heavenly bodies. All these bearings are determined by angles in relation to the movements and positions of the heavenly bodies. Again they give no clue to longitudinal displacement on northing and southing courses as the result of invisible currents, because the voyager can keep to the same angle or bearing and yet pass his objective on either side at an indefinite distance.

Bearings on horizon stars and by angles in relation to star lines were not, of course, possible during the daytime. The margin of error in supposed prehistoric navigation from and to the distant Polynesian islands entering into the conventional reconstructions would have been magnified by the fact that the sun moves continuously toward the solstices. Even if it had stood still in line with the objective, however, it would not have given the voyagers any indication of longitudinal displacement, because its distance from the earth, like that of stars that shine at night, is so great that the true courses and the false courses would have been in effect parallel. These limitations apply to the traditional course from Tahiti to New Zealand, 'a little to the left of the setting sun'.

The direction of winds, waves and ocean swells, being the same over vast tracts of ocean, give no clue to longitudinal displacement within those areas. The usual behaviour of ocean swells in the Northern Hemisphere is different from that of those in the neighbourhood of Eastern Polynesia. The Eastern Polynesian discoverers of Hawaii would have been sadly misled if they had applied their knowledge of ocean swells in their home waters to their judgment of bearings in the neighbourhood of Hawaii.

Robert C. Suggs, an American anthropologist, and Roger Duff, a New Zealand one, have suggested that the capacity of Tupaea, the Tahitian who accompanied Cook from Tahiti to Batavia via New Zealand and Australia, always to indicate the direction in which Tahiti lay, is evidence of Polynesian navigating skill.[4] The track of the *Endeavour*, however, lay

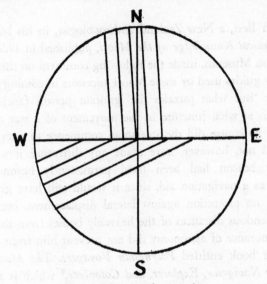

FIG. 2. Courses by Angles

Courses by angles in relation to the east-west paths of the stars and sun and the north-south lines given by the Pole Star and the Southern Cross give no clue to lateral displacement because courses intersecting such lines at the same angle are parallel with one another.

towards the west, first south and then north of the south tropic latitudes of Tahiti, so that all that Tupaea had to do, and all he could do, in order to indicate the broad easting direction in which Tahiti lay, was to point to the rising quarter of the south tropic stars. In order to check on the bearings of Tahiti in relation to the *Endeavour*, the European navigators, on each occasion that Tupaea pointed in the direction of Tahiti, would have had to calculate them by trigonometry from the latitude and longitude of the *Endeavour* and the latitude and longitude of Tahiti. Had Tupaea been given the exact bearings of Tahiti, and set out to sail there, he would have had no knowledge of the lateral displacements that would thereafter have occurred as the result of set with currents and miscalculations of drift with winds.

Elsdon Best, a New Zealand anthropologist, in his book *The Astronomical Knowledge of the Maori*, published in 1922 by the Dominion Museum, made the following comment on the alleged heavenly guides used by some Maori ancestors in coming to New Zealand: 'But what puzzles the ignorant person (such as the writer) is at what juncture in the movement of a star or other body on its course did the steersman commence to steer by it.'[5] It would not, however, have made any difference if a special heavenly beacon had been fixed permanently beyond New Zealand as a navigation aid, since it would still have given the voyagers no protection against lateral displacement, because of the tremendous distances of the heavenly bodies from the earth. Best's ignorance of astronomy did not prevent him from writing a further book entitled *Polynesian Voyagers. The Maori as a Deep-sea Navigator, Explorer, and Colonizer*,[6] which is a standard traditionalist text!

Harold Gatty, an expert in modern navigation, had a special theory of Polynesian long navigation by stars. He concluded that voyagers came within fifty to seventy-five miles of a distant objective by bringing stars overhead which were supposedly known from previous probes to be overhead at an objective at a given time of the year and a given time of the night; and that they completed the journey to their objective by the use of natural homing aids such as cloud effects, birds, and the smell of land. This theory, which has been propagated far and wide in Gatty's book *Nature is Your Guide*,[7] is based on a misunderstanding of the facts of astronomy. The times of night when a star is overhead at various points as it completes an apparent circuit of the earth are all virtually the same, the only variations being the negligible ones arising from the difference between sidereal and solar time. The margin of error in Gatty's theory, therefore, is not seventy-five miles, but the width of the Pacific

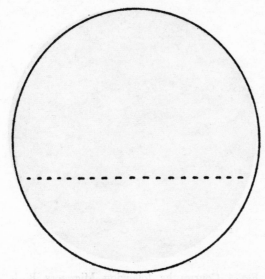

FIG. 3. The Time of Night when a Star is Overhead

The time of night when a star is overhead gives no clue to lateral displacement because a star is overhead at virtually the same time of night at every point on a parallel of latitude as the star makes an apparent circuit of the earth. The time of night is not specific to locality.

Ocean, and his argument that the voyagers, having come within fifty to seventy-five miles of their objective, used natural homing aids to make their final landfall, is beside the point. In any case Gatty, like many others, exaggerates the applicability of these aids. Cloud effects are not always present over islands, and are frequently simulated over tracts of ocean where no land exists. Releasing tropic birds as pointers to the direction of land is likely to be misleading when one has no way of knowing whether one is closer to Australia than to New Zealand, or to Micronesia than to Hawaii. Concentrations of sea-birds are not always present near land, and are discernible only in the vicinity when they are. The smell of land on the surface of the sea is

FIG. 4. Courses by following Migratory Birds

Courses by following migratory birds give no clue to lateral displacement because migratory birds are not affected by currents at night but surface craft are. The diagram represents prehistoric navigators looking for migratory birds at night.

detectable only when one is close to land, and only when the wind is blowing off the shore. Vague statements that the Polynesians sailed by these aids overlook their local character.

Gatty and others have also suggested that for long distance navigation the Polynesians found a natural aid in the following of migratory birds. But this theory is discredited by the fact that, to keep in touch with the birds in the face of set with currents and drift with winds, it would be necessary to see some of them every hour or two. In the hours of darkness at sea, however, birds are invisible, and are heard only intermittently, if at all, particularly when it is windy. Currents keep on flowing all night and every night, but birds fly on independently.

Another theory put forward by Gatty and others is that the Polynesians noted the stars which passed overhead from east to west in the latitudes of their discoveries; returned to the latitudes of their home islands and moved east or west to them by following known stars which passed overhead in those latitudes; and found their discoveries again by making northings or southings to their latitudes and then moving east or west to them by following the stars which, according to the observations made at the time of discovery, passed overhead in those latitudes. The experimental voyager Eric de Bisschop added a refinement to his version of this theory by suggesting that the voyagers, on initial exploratory probes to the north and south and back again, noted that they had been displaced by currents in relation to the home islands.[8] But he did not explain how they could have known the operation of currents outside the zone in which the home islands lay. A recent map of the Pacific, published by the National Geographic Society, Washington, shows five belts of currents in the Polynesian area extending from the Southern Cooks and Australs to Hawaii, and an area of variable currents round New Zealand.[9] The *Pacific Islands Pilot* testifies to the variations of the currents in the Polynesian area.[10] De Bisschop, with considerable ingenuity, also worked out round courses whereby Eastern Polynesian navigators could have sailed with favourable winds to Hawaii and back and to New Zealand and back (see Figure 5). This type of theory, however, does not explain how the discoverers of Hawaii and New Zealand could have acquired the sophisticated regional knowledge of longitudes, currents and winds which its proponents suppose. The only way in which the problem of longitudinal determination implicit in this type of theory could be evaded would be by the added unrealistic assumption that the

discoverers, having deduced that their apparent courses on their
outward voyages to their discoveries were subject to an indefinite
and unknown margin of longitudinal error, deliberately sailed
so far to the east of their home islands on the return journey
that the unknown longitudinal error on the outward voyage and

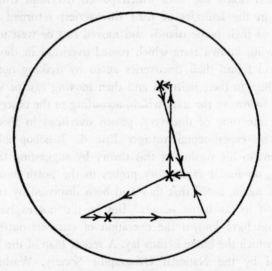

FIG. 5. Long Northing or Southing Courses followed by
Courses along Parallels of Latitude

The theory that Polynesians sailed to and from Hawaii and
New Zealand by making northings or southings to windward of their objectives and then making landfalls along
lines of latitude does not explain how the discoverers of
Hawaii and New Zealand gained the knowledge of relative
longitudes and of currents which this theory presupposes.

the return voyage was allowed for; and on each subsequent visit
to their discovery repeated this process, allowing throughout
these processes for the added margin of unknown longitudinal
error induced by any storms that overtook them.

In 1924, G. H. Heyen, on his way to San Francisco in a sailing
ship, sailed from Mangaia in the Southern Cooks to Hawaii

with the prevailing winds slightly forward of the beam (middle point) on his right or starboard side, without needing to correct his course for lateral deviation. In a recent article he pictures Eastern Polynesian navigators as sailing in the same fashion to Hawaii across the wind and returning by a similar course to Eastern Polynesia.[11]

Heyen, however, was not on a prehistoric voyage of discovery. He was making for San Francisco, and knew of its existence in advance. He therefore travelled north from Eastern Polynesia for a distance of over 2,000 miles without any thought that, if there was no land on his course, he would have had to sail back again for an equivalent distance. The reason he sailed on the wind was because he wanted to make San Francisco, not because he was trying to discover land in the direction of Hawaii before he knew of its existence. Furthermore Heyen's reconstructions contain a contradiction, for he applies his theory of voyages to Hawaii across the trade winds to imagined probes from Tahiti and the Marquesas Group, which are 1,000 miles apart, and yet presumes that, whether the navigators came from Tahiti or the Marquesas Group, they would fetch Hawaii. The prehistoric Polynesian discoverers of Hawaii, however, lacked Heyen's knowledge that, if they sailed at a certain angle with the wind from Tahiti, they would find Hawaii, and if they sailed at a different angle with the wind from the Marquesas Group, they would find Hawaii. The 'natural course' from Tahiti to Hawaii was by devious one-way voyages in which westerlies as well as easterlies probably played some part. But the Polynesian group most favourably placed in relation to the prevailing winds and currents for voyages to Hawaii was the Marquesas Group; by the same token it was least favourably placed for return voyages. Heyen's reconstruction has another flaw. The early settlers of Hawaii arrived with pigs, and it is generally agreed that the Eastern Polynesians on long settlement voyages with women, pigs and other commodities used double canoes. Reasons for this view are given in the next chapter. Stone Age double canoes, however, were subject to racking strains when sailing with the wind forward of the beam. Heyen's voyage of over 2,000 miles in a modern sailing ship has no relevance to a prehistoric voyage of discovery to Hawaii.

Heyen concedes that Tahitian voyagers to New Zealand could not have sailed across the trade wind. He makes passing reference to a direct course from Tahiti by bearings on Canopus and other stars, but does not deny that these bearings give no indication of longitudinal deviation as the result of currents and miscalculations of drift with the variable winds which lie between Eastern Polynesia and New Zealand. (The determination of longitude is a greater problem than Heyen thinks, for he endorses Gatty's erroneous view that the time when a star is overhead gives an indication of longitude, but suggests that there would have been errors when the voyagers failed to keep accurate account of dates.) Heyen then states that 'it would appear that direct voyages from Tahiti, although theoretically possible, would be beyond the capabilities of the old native navigators'. He is determined, however, to get the navigators to New Zealand and back at all costs, for he immediately makes the further suggestion that 'if contact had already been established between the island groups' the navigation to New Zealand would have been easier through Tonga or Rarotonga or both. This suggestion begs the whole question of how the discoverers of New Zealand found out the relative positions of New Zealand and Tahiti, let alone Tonga and Rarotonga. Heyen examines the possibility that navigators on return journeys from New Zealand to Tahiti sailed to the east with the aid of westerlies and then came back to their objective by a slantwise northing course with the trade wind. He concedes that the judgment of longitudes involved in such a course would constitute a problem, but does not explain how the discoverers of New Zealand could have acquired the sophisticated regional knowledge of the wind systems which his suggestion supposes.

J. Bollons, captain of the New Zealand Government steamer

Tutanekai, in the twenties of the present century wrote an article opposing the conventional views of Polynesian long navigation, although, like Cook, he confined his attention to settlement by waifs of the storm.[12] B. Hilder is another modern Pacific navigator who has achieved detachment from the knowledge derived from two centuries of Pacific exploration with instruments.[13]

Recent articles by G. S. Parsonson, a New Zealand historian, and G. M. Dening, an Australian one, are examples of the morass of futile disputation to which students who do not understand the relevant facts of physical geography condemn themselves.[14]

For Parsonson a study of wind and wave determines whether the objective is to the west or east; the problem of longitude is thus solved retrospectively for the benefit of prehistoric voyagers. Elsewhere Parsonson takes his voyagers to their destinations by bearings on stars without mentioning that these bearings give no clue to longitudinal displacement. European one-way boat voyages with instruments ranging from compasses to sextants and chronometers, made in the direction of objectives known to the voyagers, are for Parsonson indirect evidence of prehistoric navigating skill, although despite their foreknowledge of the positions of their objectives and their navigation aids, few of the voyagers managed to maintain their courses to their desired objectives.

Both Parsonson and Dening are impressed by the possibility that prehistoric voyagers followed birds both by day and by night. Both also suggest paradoxically that two-way contacts over relatively short distances in early historical times are evidence of prehistoric two-way contacts with distant islands. The many people who, like Parsonson and Dening, cite authenticated Tongan and Tahitian voyages of several hundred miles as evidence that navigation to and from distant islands was possible overlook the fact that because bearings on stars give no clue to longitudinal displacement, and the sun is a poor guide on any course without precision instruments, primitive navigation

was fundamentally a dead reckoning system depending on inti-
mate knowledge of the local geography, currents and winds, and
that all this knowledge had to be acquired by long experience
within the area where the voyages were made.

As soon as a latter-day mariner sets out in the general direction of a distant island, either in a modern vessel or one of
reconstructed Stone Age type, he puts a gulf between himself and
a prehistoric voyager, because he is applying foreknowledge of
the location of his objective in relation to his starting point.

So far little has been said of Polynesian navigation on west-
east and east-west courses, since the traditionalist reconstructions
involve long northing and southing courses. Polynesian two-way
contacts between islands west and east of each other recorded
at the time of early European exploration were comparatively
short. The most spectacular were between Tonga and Fiji (220
miles), Tahiti and the western sector of the Tahitian islands
(100 miles), and the Tahitian islands and the Tuamotu Group
(180-230 miles).

On west-east and east-west courses, the voyagers could gauge
their broad direction at night by keeping their vessels in line
with the east-west path of stars which passed overhead in that
latitude. Since they knew in advance that their destination was
east or west of their starting point, they were not subject to the
fundamental dilemma of the navigator on northing or southing
courses. The judgment of the overhead point of a star, however,
is subject to a margin of error ranging from the equivalent on
the surface of the sea of at least thirty miles to sixty miles even
on the deck of a modern steamer, and must have been just as
difficult from a Stone Age canoe. During the day, moreover,
the navigator had to sail by the sun, which is a poor navigation
guide, since it is seldom that its rising, zenith and setting points
are favourably placed for a desired course. The most serious
obstacle to systematic west-east and east-west two-way contacts
in the central belt of Polynesian islands, however, was the fact
that the prevailing winds were easterly, and the seasonal wester-

Original by John Webber, artist on Cook's third voyage. Stone Age double canoes tied together with vegetable fibres were subject to racking strains when sailing with the wind forward of the beam. They were, however, suitable for settlement voyages with the wind on the quarter, being stable and capacious.

lies of the summer months were fitful. More is said of the effects
of these meteorological conditions in Chapter Three.

Much ingenuity has been expended by various theorists on
devising primitive instruments whereby prehistoric navigators
might have judged the altitudes of stars as guides to latitude.
There is no documentation of the use of any of them in the
records of early European observers. The Polynesians had little
need for sticks or other devices on their authenticated west-east
and east-west voyages between wide screens of islands.

In the twenties of the present century, an American admiral
became convinced that a sacred calabash in Hawaii had been
used in former times for determining latitude, since when the
Pole Star was viewed through two holes in it, its altitude corresponded to the latitude of Hawaii.[15] An ethnologist of Hawaii
has shown that the calabash was in fact a receptacle for carrying
things.[16] It has also been suggested that the sun's altitude at
noon at a given time of the year was measured by the shadow
cast by an upright stick, thereby giving a record of the latitude
of the place where the observation was made.[17] Since, however,
the sun continuously shifts from north or south to the next solstice, and time at sea is relative, it is difficult to see how the
navigators could have equated the dates of their later observations to those of the original records, particularly on long
voyages. Sticks, like calabash or coconut quadrants, would have
been of no use in determining longitude on northing or southing
courses.

Both on westing and easting courses and on southing and
northing ones, the guidance given to Polynesian voyagers by
their methods of sailing on short voyages by identifiable stars
would not have been increased by their undoubted awareness
of star patterns and relationships over the entire visible sky as it
appeared to rotate above them. On westing and easting courses
identifiable stars gave indications of the lines of latitude along
which the desired courses lay, and no added guidance would
have been given by an awareness of other stars and star patterns.

D

On northing and southing courses direction-finding by an
awareness of star patterns and relationships over a wide tract
of sky is at bottom based on a combination of bearings on constellations or stars which are supposedly in line with the objective and bearings by angles in relation to other constellations or
stars; these bearings all become simultaneously erroneous when
longitudinal deviation occurs, for the reasons indicated in
Figures 1 and 2.

It has been suggested that if distant islands were not picked
up at first, they could have been found by deliberate search.[18]
On long journeys, however, primitive voyagers had no precise
means of determining the distance they had come. All that
they could do was to estimate distance by average sailing time.
The farther they went, the greater the probability of error. How
then would they have known when to search, or where? They
would have had no idea whether their objective was to their
right or their left, or how far to go in one direction before
changing to another. Since one piece of ocean looks much like
another, they might have searched the same part over again
without knowing it. Nor can the difficulties be overcome by
imagining fleets of canoes fanning out to increase the range of
visibility on long voyages. How could the vessels have kept in
touch at night, particularly during squalls? The ocean is too
deep for anchors. Even in the daylight hours the voyagers would
have had to keep within sight or sound of one another, so that
ten canoes which might be imagined as having kept in touch
despite all the difficulties would have increased the range of
vision by only forty or fifty miles.

Several records give evidence of the difficulty of finding ocean
islands, even when they are relatively near at hand and their
approximate location is known.

When John Williams made his first attempt from Aitutaki to
reach Rarotonga 146 miles to the south, he knew its broad direction and distance from some Rarotongans who had been brought

to Aitutaki by a European whaler, and who accompanied him on his search.[19] His ship had a mast and a telescope. Despite these advantages Williams and his men looked for Rarotonga for a week without success, and then gave up. Yet Rarotonga is an island with high points.

The Tahitian missionaries, who, through accidental voyagers from Manihiki to Aitutaki, knew of Manihiki, 600 miles north of Aitutaki, looked repeatedly for the island for many years before they finally made contact with it in 1849.[20]

Again, the Spaniards on Guam, 300 miles north of the Western Caroline Group, learnt of the direction and approximate distance of these islands from accidental voyagers to Guam, and from a Spanish ship which had seen them by accident. The Spanish authorities sent a ship to look for the islands, which are numerous. The ship sought for them for nearly a month without seeing any, and the search was given up for another decade.[21]

We have stressed in our analysis the effects of currents and miscalculations of drift with winds in upsetting the dead reckoning of Polynesian discoverers. In doing so we have assumed that the discoverers attempted to keep account of their courses on their voyages of discovery, and that the weather remained fine. These assumptions are highly questionable. Discoverers who had been blown away and had lost their bearings while attempting to settle local islands would obviously have had only the vaguest idea of their courses on their voyages of discovery. In the case of voluntary exiles or supposed explorers, the thought that attempts were made to sustain their dead reckoning by day and by night over great distances is likewise unrealistic, particularly if storms occurred. Another hazard would have been the obscuration of the sky by storm clouds or fog.

Evidence of the effect of loss of sky visibility is given in one of Mariner's stories.[22] After the wreck of his ship in Tonga, he salvaged a small compass. On one occasion he was making a voyage with Finau, a chief of Tonga. They were overtaken by fog, and the navigators took their line from the direction of the wind as it was at the time when the stars were lost to sight. From the compass Mariner saw that the wind had changed, and that if the vessel continued on its course with the changed wind, it would miss its destination. He prevailed on Finau, on pledge of his life, to let him give the steering directions, reckoning that otherwise he was lost anyway. Mariner changed course and went on all night. One may imagine the tension. But with the dawn, their destination showed up ahead. Finau was so pleased with the white man's magic that he used the compass on every occasion afterwards, whether necessary or not. (Since Mariner could not explain satisfactorily why the needle pointed north, Finau's firm opinion was that it was kept there by a special god.)

Compare this story with a statement by Robert C. Suggs that he was converted to a faith in Polynesian navigating ability in former times when Louis Tapoto, a modern Tahitian captain, on a trip from the Marquesas Group to Takaroa, some 440 miles away, successfully maintained his dead reckoning despite loss of sky visibility during which the wind boxed the compass.[23] Tapoto's feat, however, has no relevance to non-instrumental navigation, because a compass, being like an eye which sees the north in the dark, makes it possible to know the broad direction of a vessel's course and the direction in which to lay off leeway in dead reckoning when the wind changes in obscure weather. The fact that Tapoto and other modern navigators in that area are adept in judging the vagaries of set and drift merely proves that, even with instruments, local knowledge acquired over many years is essential for dead reckoning.

Although in the days before navigation instruments deliberate navigation to and from distant ocean islands was impossible in any form of sailing or paddling craft, the Polynesians deserve their reputation as outstanding voyagers. The Europeans who observed their journeys of several hundred miles in the Tonga-Samoa-Fiji and Tahiti-Tuamotu areas, knowing something of navigation difficulties in the days of sail, even with quadrants, compasses and charts, were continually amazed at the Polynesians' feats of seamanship and daring. But later Europeans were apparently not impressed with anything less than the idea of two-way voyages of a thousand miles and more. It is the sophisticated Europeans, with their Mercator's projection, their navigation instruments, and their accumulated knowledge from two centuries of Pacific exploration with these aids, who have forgotten the fundamental limitations of primitive navigation.

Most people believe what they want to believe, and most people want to believe that the Polynesians sailed back and forth to their distant islands without quadrant, compass or chart. If and when the fallacies inherent in the prevailing views of Polynesian navigation to and from those islands become more apparent, there will no doubt be an increase in statements that we do not know the methods of prehistoric Polynesian navigation, and in suggestions that they navigated by a mysterious instinct or sixth sense.[24] The prehistoric Polynesians, however, could not extract from the facts of nature more than was in them. The view that they were supermen is not a satisfactory basis for a theory of Polynesian long navigation.

CHAPTER THREE

STONE AGE VESSELS IN THE PACIFIC

THE limitations on the range of Polynesian two-way navigation reviewed in Chapter Two would have applied to any form of sailing or paddling vessel which the Polynesians might have used. The types of vessels employed by them and by other people in the Pacific are a matter of interest in themselves, and also have a bearing on the manner of the Polynesian migrations.

Of Polynesian craft in historical times, there is a considerable amount of evidence in the accounts of early European observers.[1] This evidence shows that the Polynesian sea-going vessels were canoes with single outriggers, and double canoes consisting of two hulls fastened together with connecting booms. Rafts were used in Mangareva and elsewhere, but they were merely assemblages of logs and bamboo canes, used for local transport and lacking centreboards with which they could come into the wind.

Of the winds by which the Tongans and Tahitians sailed on their voyages of up to several hundred miles in historical times, there is also ample evidence in the accounts of early Europeans. W. T. Pritchard recorded that the Tongans, on their voyages to and from Samoa, sailed across the south-east trade wind both going and coming, but that on their voyages to Fiji, which lay to the west, they went with the trade wind, and then, in order to get back to their own islands, awaited the seasonal westerlies which blow sporadically in the summer months.[2] When Dillon visited Rotuma, he cited as evidence of the existence of a 'north-west or west monsoon' the fact that a European ship sailed without tacking, from the equator to Samoa, by the aid of westerly and north-westerly winds.[3] In Tahiti, Anderson, Cook's associate whose observations were cited in Chapter One, was told that the Tahitians, on their visits to the western sector of their group, waited for the westerlies of the summer months in order to get back over the hundred miles separating the western and eastern sectors.[4] Morrison, one of the *Bounty* mutineers, found that the Tahitians came down to Mehetia with a north wind and waited there for the wind to change in order to run with the south-east trade wind to the Tuamotus.[5]

The character of Polynesian voyaging is further shown by Mariner's accounts of Tongan voyages.[6] Occasionally a Tongan chief would go off and join in the Fijian wars. One chief, after spending two years in Fiji, came back to Tonga, but lost a canoe with some of his best men on the voyage. Another chief, Kau Moala, told Mariner that after adventuring in Fiji for a couple of years, he decided to come home. In due course he sighted Vavau, in the north of the Tonga Group. He could not make land because of the wind, and therefore decided to run for Samoa, a long way to the north-east. He could not make Samoa either, and ran west to Futuna, some distance to the north-west of Tonga. The people of Futuna knew no country other than their own, and had no large canoes. After a year Kau Moala decided to push off for Fiji. He came west to Rotuma, where the people treated him as a god, having never seen so large a canoe as his. He again set off for Fiji, taking with him some Rotumans. Yet again he was taken off course by winds, but managed to make Fiji. Here he joined again in the local wars as the ally of one of the Fijian factions. Finally he got back to Tonga.

Dillon's evidence, gathered a decade or so later, shows that he found Rotumans scattered as far east as Samoa and as far west as Tikopia, and was told of a Tongan expedition which had set out for Rotuma and never been heard of since.[7] It is indeed plain that it was only in a limited sense that Rotuma could have been described as being in systematic two-way contact with other islands.

William Ellis, a contemporary of Dillon, made several voyages in Tahitian double canoes. He said that in fine weather and with a favourable wind the canoes were tolerably safe and comfortable, but that when the weather was rough and the winds contrary they were 'tossed about completely at the mercy of the winds'.[8]

The evidence of early European observers that the Polynesian voyagers in early historical times preferred to await the seasonal westerlies rather than to beat against the prevailing winds and currents on west-east passages of 100 to 200 miles is in conformity with common sense. Tests with models of oceanic sailing canoes by C. O. Bechtol, an American experimenter, show that both double canoes and outrigger canoes can sail with reasonable efficiency against the wind provided they have sufficient steep wetted surface to resist leeway, either in the form of V-bottoms or large steering oars used as leeboards.[9] In the case of sailing canoes with single outriggers, this fact was documented by Kotzebue and L. C. de Freycinet[10] at the time of early European contact with Micronesia. Freycinet commented, however, that these vessels were liable to be overset when sailing close to the wind, and both he and Kotzebue graphically described the procedures of the crews in righting them when this happened. Stone Age outrigger canoes, moreover, were tied together with vegetable fibres, and therefore more vulnerable to stress than modern sailing craft, or than modern outrigger canoes shaped with iron tools and fastened together with bolts or nails. Stone Age double canoes were more stable than outrigger canoes, but were a great deal more vulnerable to stress when sailing against the wind, because their two hulls were fastened together with booms bound with vegetable fibres. When sailing vessels are going with the wind and the run of the seas the stresses are less severe. As Bechtol points out, even modern yachts avoid upwind courses as far as possible. Furthermore there is a point in the force of a wind at which no sailing vessel can make headway upwind, as the evidence of the early European observers of Tongan and Tahitian voyages shows.

In the light of the evidence that the Polynesians waited for the westerlies of the summer months in order to sail over the short distances between Fiji and Tonga and the western and eastern sectors of the Tahitian islands, it is highly unrealistic to imagine that explorers from the west in prehistoric times fought against the trade winds for distances of 500 to 2,000 miles in order to find islands they did not know existed.

An erroneous belief of many writers on Polynesian voyaging is that a vessel which is fast when running with the wind is for that reason suitable for ocean voyages. Double canoes and single outrigger canoes are particularly fast when running. Tacking into the wind, however, is an entirely different proposition from running with it, because of the greater difficulty of making headway, and also because of the strains on the vessels. Another frequent error is the assumption that because a vessel is tacking into the wind, it is making headway against the wind. In fact such a vessel may be gaining very little on the wind.

The difficulties of pitting double canoes against the adverse winds that are a constant risk on long ocean journeys are not resolved by thinking that they could have been helped substantially on their way by the use of paddles. If the freeboard had been low enough for paddles to be used with any great effect, the canoes would have been vulnerable to swamping by heavy seas. Their broad beam, moreover, meant that a great deal of sustained effort would have been required to keep them moving against wind and sea. On the other hand huge canoes would have had difficulties of another kind, since one hull would have been hanging half in and half out of the water as each wave was mounted. The most efficient sea-going double canoes were probably of medium size.

Canoes with single outriggers, though liable to capsize when a sudden gust hit the lee side of the sail, or when the outrigger came up too high, were reasonably stable when paddled with the sail down and the outrigger in the water. If, however, the freeboard had been low enough for efficient paddling, it would have been insufficient to prevent shipping of water in heavy seas, and the vessel's carrying capacity would have been small.

Canoes with single outriggers, either with or without sails, could have been the means of peopling uninhabited islands after being blown away in storms. For the reasons just given, however, it is doubtful whether they played any appreciable part in settlement by voluntary exiles.

We come back, then, to the double canoe as the presumptive major instrument of the one-way settlement of the farther islands of Polynesia. It was well suited to the role, being stable because of its broad beam, and capable of covering long distances when running with the wind, although not when beating or being paddled against it. Even a medium-sized double canoe could have carried a considerable cargo of human beings, animals, plants, water, food, and other commodities.

Most Pacific ethnologists have been content to assume that the Polynesian ancestors brought with them, as their sea-going vessels, double canoes and single canoes with outriggers, such as were found in historical times not only in Polynesia, but also in Melanesia and Micronesia. Not so, however, the experimental voyagers Eric de Bisschop and Thor Heyerdahl.

De Bisschop believed that the Polynesians came into their islands from the west, and interested himself in the vessels whereby they might have accomplished this. In Hawaii he constructed a two-hulled vessel using modern tools, joinery and metalwork—including steel springs to reduce the racking strains on the connexions between the hulls, large sawn beams for keel plates, and nuts, bolts, and nails. There was, of course, a considerable difference between this craft and a Stone Age double canoe fastened with vegetable fibres. De Bisschop decided to visit the north-east corner of the Pacific in this vessel. On its trials he was able to get only four miles to windward against strong winds during the whole of a sleepless night. He then decided not to visit the north-east corner of the Pacific, but to sail in a westing direction for France. He succeeded in this feat, travelling for the most part with the trade winds and currents. On the way he made observations of migratory birds as a potential navigation aid and formed a contempt for the notion that prehistoric voyagers followed them. Later de Bisschop tried out a sailing canoe of Philippine Islands type, with outriggers on each side like the Philippine Islands craft. He had a good opinion of its sailing qualities, but thought it unsuitable for long colonizing voyages because of its restricted carrying capacity. He had a poor opinion of sailing canoes with single outriggers for such voyages, because of their unsuitability for carrying large loads of people and goods, and their tendency, already remarked on, to be overset when the wind suddenly changes to the opposite side from the outrigger.[11]

Eventually de Bisschop and Heyerdahl fastened on rafts as their preferred craft for bringing Polynesians to distant destinations. Heyerdahl pictured the prehistoric colonists as coming from the Americas with the prevailing winds, and emulated them in practice on his Kon-Tiki raft.[12] It was his hope that he would find out the lost secret of how the Inca sailors of the eighteenth century made their balsa rafts come into the wind with the aid of planks thrust down into the water between the logs as centreboards. But if rafts with centreboards could sail upwind, de Bisschop argued, they could have conveyed Polynesians from west to east.

When Thor Heyerdahl succeeded in reaching Eastern Polynesia from Peru on a balsa raft with multiple centreboards inserted between the logs, de Bisschop, according to a statement he made later, was astonished that, whereas the Spaniards Juan and Ulloa, in 1736, had said that the Incas made their rafts work against the wind by manipulating their moveable centreboards, Heyerdahl's centreboards had been fixed in the first place.[13] Certain it is that in due course Heyerdahl learned the secret of sailing against the wind by manipulating moveable centre-boards.[14]

De Bisschop set out in 1956 from Tahiti to America on a bamboo raft with moveable centreboards in an effort to demonstrate that the Polynesians went to America and back in such craft. He argued that rafts with moveable centreboards, though slow, would have been the best craft for long colonizing expeditions, because they were stable, immune from leaks, and big enough to carry the loads involved. He did not attempt to beat against the trade wind and current to America, but went down to latitude 35° S. and thereabouts, where westerly winds are frequent and occasional east-setting currents occur. He proved, as Heyerdahl had done, that rafts with moveable centreboards could make some headway against the wind. After six months he was slightly east of Juan Fernandez, over 3,000 miles from Tahiti and less than 300 miles from America, when his raft broke up and he was rescued by a Chilean vessel.[15]

Nothing daunted, de Bisschop and some companions set out from Peru on an attempted return journey to Tahiti on a balsa raft with moveable centreboards. After two months the raft started to become waterlogged and could not make the Tuamotus because the winds and currents carried it too far north. De Bisschop and his companions had to abandon the balsa raft and take to an improvised raft of water drums and timber. After nearing various islands and then being borne away from them by changing currents and winds, the makeshift vessel was wrecked on a reef at Rakahanga in the Northern Cooks, where de Bisschop suffered fatal injuries.[16]

De Bisschop did not die in vain. He was a modern Columbus who demonstrated things different from those he set out to prove. He threw light on the difficulties and rarity of long easting voyages in the trade wind zone in prehistoric times, made either by intent or accident, and the still greater difficulties of two-way voyages from Polynesia to America, even with navigation instruments. He also concluded from first-hand observations that there was no wisdom in trying to follow migratory birds on long ocean voyages. Finally he demonstrated the variability of ocean currents in the Polynesian area.

If some or all of the Polynesian ancestors came into the Pacific from the west, the westerlies of the summer months would have enabled them to do so in vessels no more efficient than those they were using at the time of European contact. These westerlies blow fitfully all the way from the East Indies to Eastern Polynesia. Because they are unpredictable, often intermittent, and frequently violent, however, they would have been unreliable for systematic long voyaging from west to east. These same characteristics made the summer westerlies highly suitable for initiating a slow succession of one-way voyages of settlement from west to east.

CHAPTER FOUR

VOYAGES OF NO RETURN

THE first European after Cook to move fairly systematically round the islands of the central belt of Polynesia and leave a full account was John Williams, the head of the London Missionary Society's post in Raiatea, in the western sector of the Tahitian islands, from 1817 to 1839.[1] Trained as a craftsman, he was a man of practical bent. While stranded at Rarotonga for a year, he built a small schooner which he called *Messenger of Peace*. When the vessel was ready, Williams and a Rarotongan chief and a crew of enthusiastic Rarotongans sailed to Aitutaki, 146 miles to the north.[2] This was the first time the chief had ever been to sea. Williams had a quadrant and a compass and knew the position of Aitutaki, so this time he landed on his target, which was different from what had happened previously when he tried to find Rarotonga from Aitutaki, and had to give up after searching for a week. After two trips from Raiatea to Tonga and Samoa, Williams met his death at the hands of the natives of Eromanga, in the New Hebrides.[3]

The notes Williams left of various one-way voyages which came to his notice give an invaluable and dramatic picture of their potentiality for one-way settlement.[4]

Manihiki and Rakahanga are two atolls about twenty-five miles apart in the Northern Cooks, some 600 miles north of Aitutaki. When Williams set up a mission station on Aitutaki, he learned of the existence of Manihiki because some lost voyagers from there had arrived on Aitutaki about sixty years previously.

Later, Williams received more information about Manihiki, and also Rakahanga, from some one-way voyagers. One of the native missionaries on Rurutu, some 1,000 miles south-east of

Manihiki, had a small European sail-boat. Some Americans had come to Rurutu, and the missionary, accompanied by his wife and some Rurutuans, set out with the visitors for Tahiti, about 350 miles north. The boat was caught in a storm and the destination was missed. Six weeks later the voyagers sighted a low island, from which some canoes came out to the boat. The people in them said that the island was Manihiki. The Americans and one or two of the Rurutuans decided to make contact with the local chief to see if they could get supplies. Before they returned a gale came up and swept the boat away to the north. Another atoll, Rakahanga, then came in sight. The missionary and his wife and the remaining Rurutuans landed and found the native huts left just as if the people were all out visiting. There were even some human heads with flowing black hair. The Manihiki-Rakahanga custom was to live on one island at a time, letting the fish and vegetation recover on the other. At that time the islanders were on Manihiki, so Rakahanga was deserted. The voyagers stocked up with food and pushed off again, as any of us would no doubt have done in the same circumstances. They had no notion where they were heading, but the prevailing winds and currents decided that it should be to Niuatobutabu, in the north of the Tonga Group, 1,000 miles west of Manihiki. Here they were received with kindness after their wanderings of over 2,000 miles. Some time later, Williams visited Tonga, where he heard that a native missionary was working at Niuatobutabu. He went there and found the wife of the missionary from Rurutu, the husband having died a short time before. Williams heard the whole story from the lady, who told him that the Manihikians were like the Tuamotuans.

There is a loose string in this story, which is as dramatic as any in the long annals of the sea. What happened to the Americans who were left stranded on Manihiki when the boat left? When Williams heard about them from the survivors, he hoped that they would sow the seed of the Gospel in Manihiki. But when the island was found by the mission ship ten years after

Williams's death, no sign of them remained. The island's existence was again revealed when a ship found a lost canoe containing another pathetic little company who had been blown away
from Manihiki. With this further clue, the missionaries, who had
searched repeatedly for the island over a period of years, finally
found it, nearly thirty years after its existence first became known
to Williams. In the years that followed, canoes were often blown
away while passing between Manihiki and Rakahanga. Yet the
islands were only twenty-five miles apart. The missionaries
finally persuaded the people to give up their migrations between
the two atolls and settle each separately.[5]

From Raivavae, on the southern fringe of Polynesia, an epic
one-way voyage occurred during Williams's time in Polynesia.
A vessel with a number of people was carried to the west. As
the weeks went by, the toll of the dead mounted to twenty. After
three long months, land showed up ahead. This was Manua, in
the Samoa Group, some 1,500 miles from Raivavae. Williams
happened to come across the survivors of this voyage on one of
his two visits to Western Polynesia.

On one of his trips to the west, Williams found still another
lot of one-way voyagers. This time it was some Aitutakians who
had been carried for 1,000 miles to Niuafou, north-west of the
main Tongan islands. Williams came as the Good Samaritan
who took them home.

Williams was in Polynesia for the space of only one generation. The Polynesians had been there a hundred times longer.
Yet during his relatively brief sojourn, the one-way voyages
which came to his notice ranged from Rurutu in the south to
Manihiki 1,000 miles north; from Manihiki to Aitutaki 600
miles south; and from Eastern Polynesia to Western Polynesia
over distances of up to 1,500 miles. We can only guess how many
more one-way voyagers were borne to distant islands during
Williams's time in the Pacific.

One point that will not have failed to attract the attention of
those who remember the prevailing easterly winds, and the cur-

A View from Savaii

rents that flow from the east, is that though some of the voyagers
in Williams's stories went south, others north, and most west,
none of them came from west to east. Nevertheless Williams
believed that the Polynesians came from the west in the first
place. He himself sailed for considerable distances from west to
east in the Polynesian area with the aid of westerlies, and concluded that the Polynesian ancestors could have come from the
west by the same means.

Other early European observers in the Pacific also recorded
instances of one-way voyages. For example, when Dillon visited
Tonga in the early nineteenth century, he was told by a chief
that a canoe from Aitutaki had finished up on one of the Tongan
islands with five survivors out of ten passengers after having
been lost at sea for five months.[6]

William Ellis, the early missionary in the Tahitian islands,
recorded similar incidents in his books published in 1827 and
1831.[7] Thus he wrote of the surprise that awaited the first missionary to visit the lonely island of Rapa, located far to the
south of the central belt of Polynesian islands. He found there
a man named 'Mapuagua' who had arrived twelve years before
from Mangareva, with six other people, including women. They
had been blown away in a storm, and had come on a raft with
the winds and currents from the east for a distance of over 600
miles. These people were among the luckiest voyagers ever projected into the Pacific wastes, because Rapa is only five miles
wide, with no islands on either side or beyond for a very great
distance.

Ellis also mentions a voyage from the Tuamotuan island of
Hao to Tahiti, which brought the Tahitians of that time knowledge of this island which they had not had before, and another
voyage from Tahiti to one of the islands in the Southern Cooks.
These were evidently one-way voyages, for Ellis said that com-
parable voyages in the reverse or eastern direction were unknown to him. He also reported a voyage by a chief in a very
large canoe from Rurutu to Tahiti, which he suggested had

E

taken somewhat longer than a direct course; a voyage in the reverse direction from Tahiti to Rurutu, a smaller target, would have been much more difficult.

Ellis tells of later voyages by Tahitians to and from islands in the Austral Group several hundred miles south of the Tahitian islands, in European-style vessels, but by that time the courses had been established by Europeans and compasses had been introduced.

Since all the voyages that Ellis knew of were from east to west, he thought that some of the Polynesian ancestors might have come from America, the prevailing winds and currents being from that direction.[8]

A number of European observers after Ellis testified to the potentialities of one-way voyages for settlement. Sheldon Dibble, a missionary in the Hawaiian Islands from 1830, suggested that the Polynesians had been distributed round the Pacific in that way.[9]

George Turner, one of the first white missionaries to live permanently in Samoa, visited Rotuma in 1845. There he saw twenty people, both men and women, who had been picked up by a whaling vessel after being blown away from the Gilberts, several hundred miles north-east of Rotuma. Turner cited this as an example of the way islands were settled, saying that had these people come on an uninhabited island, they would have called it after their home island and settled there.[10]

On the same trip Turner found some Tongans and Samoans on an island in the New Hebrides, many hundreds of miles west of Tonga and Samoa. They had been blown away while passing from Savaii in Samoa for Tonga. Again women were numbered among them; again it had been a one-way trip; and again they had taken up their residence where fate had led them.[11]

Another remarkable story, particularly notable as evidence that accidental journeys were occasionally made over long distances from west to east, was recounted by F. W. Beechey, the British naval commander who visited the eastern islands of Polynesia in 1824.[12] On one of the Tuamotus he found a number of people who had set off from Anaa to sail west to Tahiti three years previously. So far from reaching Tahiti, they had finished up on an uninhabited island 420 miles east of Anaa, with no knowledge of where they were. They had set out in the first place in company with two other sea-going canoes, the full party comprising 150 people of both sexes and all ages. They made good progress and were looking out for Mehetia, the easternmost Tahitian island, when a westerly gale came up. The canoes were parted and did not come together again. Beechey's informants, after being battered by the gale for some days, then encountered better weather and set sail again for the west in the hope of reaching their destination. After two more days, however, during which they did not sight land, they were becalmed for many days. They grew exhausted from paddling, and their food and water ran out, although they had taken enough for three weeks. Some of them drank sea-water. Then they began to die. The survivors in their extremity ate their dead companions' flesh, although they were not ordinarily cannibals. They managed to gaff a shark, which kept the survivors going after two dozen of the original forty-eight people in the canoe had died. Another gale came up, and was welcomed because it gave them water. This gale also was from the west. Eventually they arrived on an uninhabited Tuamotuan island nearly 600 miles east of Mehetia.

J. D. Lang, a churchman of Sydney in New South Wales, plied back and forth across the South Pacific on a number of occasions in the middle decades of the nineteenth century. He interested himself in the problem of the Polynesian migrations, and noted the frequent occurrence of westerly winds even in the tropics where the prevailing winds are easterly. He collected evidence of the types of voyages that were made by the islanders of the South Pacific, and came to the conclusion that the long ones included voyages of exiles as well as of people blown away, and were not exclusively from east to west. So impressed with the possibilities from voyages in westerlies did Lang become that he formed the theory that the Polynesians had settled America.[13]

William Wyatt Gill, a missionary who lived in the Cook Islands for twenty-two years and visited other parts of Polynesia, recorded some notable one-way voyages.[14]

When Gill visited Manua in the Samoa Group in 1862, he met some people who had come from Moorea in the Tahitian islands, a distance of 1,250 miles, with no lives lost. Another of his accounts tells of a voyage from Manihiki in the Northern Cooks to the Ellice Group north-west of Samoa. During this voyage of over 1,000 miles, half the party perished from want of food and water.

The most significant of Gill's reports tells of a voyage which bridged the gap between Western and Eastern Polynesia. Fakaofo is an island in the Tokelau Group, about 300 miles north of Samoa. In January 1858, says Gill, a 'numerous family' was conveyed from Fakaofo via the uninhabited atolls of Nassau and Palmerston to Mangaia in the Southern Cooks. This journey was over a distance of 1,250 miles, the easting component being about 700 miles. Gill pointed out the potentialities of the westerlies of the summer months for settlement from west to east.

William Pritchard, who was born in Tahiti and in the middle of the nineteenth century lived for many years in Western Polynesia and Fiji, after reviewing the legends of Fiji, Tonga, and Samoa, wrote in his book published in 1866: 'Apart from these legendary accounts, it cannot be doubted that the early migrations of the ancestors of these islands were involuntary rather than the result of roving dispositions, or the pressure of limited and over-populated homes; that, in fact, they were blown away from their earlier homes in their frail canoes.' Pritchard remarked that no voyages from west to east were known.[15]

It is clear that the controversy among the earlier European observers who saw Polynesian voyaging for themselves was over the direction from which the Polynesian ancestors came to their islands rather than over how they got there. Apart from those who thought that the facts could be explained by migration with the aid of former land connexions or chains of islands —a view which geological research has since disposed of—the early Europeans were almost unanimous in thinking that settlement across the longer gaps between the Pacific Islands had occurred by accident. Most of those who held this view, however, failed to take account of the possibilities from voyages of exiles, as Cook had failed to before them; or at least did not make specific mention of these possibilities.

The accounts of one-way voyages given in the present chapter tell of the arrival of one-way voyagers including both women and men on distant islands in the Polynesian area. The survivors of these voyages were living proof of the potentialities of one-way voyages for the settlement of Polynesia in prehistoric times.

The evidence shows that long west-east voyages in historical times were few and far between, but long east-west ones were comparatively frequent. This provides an essential key to the understanding of the reasons for cultural distributions in the Pacific Islands, as we shall see in Chapter Six.

In addition to the many recorded instances of one-way voyages over long distances made by waifs of the storm in early historical times, there is further historical evidence of one-way voyages of voluntary exiles who pushed off in the hope of finding land, and of exiles who were forced out to sea.

David Porter, an American naval commander who visited the Marquesas Group in 1813, was told that voluntary exiles frequently set off for traditional islands and were never heard of again. The grandfather of one of the chiefs of Nuku Hiva had gone off with four large canoes furnished with livestock and food plants. A European informant who had been living in the Marquesas Group for a number of years estimated that during his time there many hundreds of people had set off in this way, having been encouraged to do so by priests who told them of traditional islands.[16]

In the early nineteenth century, a Rotuman told a European visitor that larger canoes had been retained on Rotuma so that when population pressure arose, expeditions of voluntary exiles might go off in them.[17]

George Turner recorded the case of some Manihikians who, having learned from Europeans that there were islands to the west, pushed off from a daring born of ignorance to visit them, and arrived eventually in the Tokelaus to the north of Samoa.[18] Later again the missionaries on Uvea reported that similar incidents had occurred.[19] Other instances, in which young men went off on trips of self-exile from Tikopia, are on record.[20]

These records of the setting out of voluntary exiles in historical times are few compared with the prolific evidence of voyages of waifs blown away in storms, but the faith of the Polynesian in the gods would undoubtedly have been an encouragement to him on voyages of voluntary exile in pre-European times.

In addition to voyages made by voluntary exiles there is some evidence of voyages made by exiles under duress. When on one occasion the British missionaries in Tahiti fell foul of the local people, they threatened to force the missionaries out to sea.[21] It seems probable that the Polynesians sometimes did this to their enemies.

Another story which Porter heard in the Marquesas Group said that a tribe which was hard pressed in war constructed many large double canoes for the purpose of searching for other homes, but did not set out since peace was made.[22]

In 1893 a younger relative of a chief of Manihiki, being jealous of the latter's position, made preparations to go off to sea with his family, and was in due course forced to do so because he was a trouble-maker. These exiles arrived in Samoa. A. P. Vayda, an American anthropologist who drew attention to this record in 1958, pointed out that incidents of this character, coupled with defeat, or the threat of defeat, in war, could have led to voyages of exiles in prehistoric times.[23]

We may sum up the evidence, therefore, as being in favour of the view that voyages of exiles, both voluntary and forced, as well as of people blown away in storms while on local voyages, played a part in the one-way settlement of distant islands. In neither case was there deliberate navigation to defined objectives, although vague notions of other land no doubt provided a frequent incentive to voluntary exiles.

It cannot be too strongly emphasized that 'drift voyages' is a very inadequate term for voyages arising either from storms or exile. The essential feature of these voyages was that they were random, unnavigated ones. This does not mean that the voyagers lacked control of their vessels or were at the mercy of the winds and waves. When they came in sight of land they could make for it. This was exploration, although the actual sighting of land, like all discovery, came of necessity by chance.

Polynesia continues to be a field for nautical overstatements. They have recently been added to by Robert C. Suggs, in his book *The Island Civilizations of Polynesia*.[24] Citing archaeological evidence in the Marquesas Group and Hawaii that the early settlers of these groups brought with them animals and plants and other goods, Suggs concluded that the settlers arrived in sizeable expeditions of more than one canoe. The many long voyages in native craft which were recorded in Polynesia in historical times, however, were invariably made by isolated canoes. This is not surprising in view of the difficulties of retaining contact night after night on such voyages. In any case, as George Vason's experience shows, the carrying capacity of one large double canoe was great. Vason accompanied over 250 armed Tongan warriors in one double canoe at the end of the eighteenth century.[25] This human cargo represents a weight of about twenty tons, which is equivalent to that of thirty persons, two boars, three sows, twelve piglets, thirty fowls, ten dogs, twenty rats, a hundred balled or potted breadfruit and banana plants, and twelve tons of water-gourds, seeds, yams, tubers, coconuts, adzes and weapons. A double canoe one-third the size would have been ample for viable settlement.

Suggs also stated that Andrew Sharp, the author of the present book, in his earlier book, *Ancient Voyagers in the Pacific*, had advanced the theory that the Pacific Islands were settled by 'ships blown off course while fishing, and so on', 'fishermen or travellers caught in storms and blown off course'. The present author had not in fact confined his theory of settlement to fishermen or travellers blown away; he had mentioned in nine separate places in *Ancient Voyagers in the Pacific* the possibility of settlement by exiles. There is, however, no way of knowing for certain whether any island or group was settled in the first place by exiles who set out in the hope of finding new land, or by people who were blown away while attempting to settle a local island, because the preparations would be the same in each case.

In addition Suggs stated that, since there were no islands to the east of Easter Island and the Marquesas Group, there was no source from which Easter Island and the Marquesas Group could have been settled in accordance with Sharp's theory. Yet in the preceding sentence Suggs had said that west-east voyages, as well as east-west voyages, formed part of Sharp's theory.

Suggs also wondered why, if Sharp's theory were correct, there were no signs of the arrival of Polynesians on the coast of Asia. Since, however, Asia was peopled long before the Pacific Islands, any casual migrants from the Pacific Islands who were not killed off would soon have been absorbed without trace. No doubt Pacific Islanders who reached the Australian continent would have been similarly absorbed.

Finally Suggs stated that Sharp's theory explained nothing, being applicable to any area of the earth. By the same logic, as Einstein's general theory has been shown by successive tests to apply to bodies in space, it has steadily lost its power to explain anything!

Throughout the century after Cook, until the old order in Polynesia had gone for ever, we have seen evidence of a steady succession of one-way migrants to distant Polynesian islands, but not of two-way contacts between them. One century is not long, and the recorded voyages were no doubt only a fraction of those made even within that century. Yet those which attracted notice could have colonized the central belt of Polynesian islands, no less from the west than from the east. Extend the time back for twenty to thirty centuries, and any other explanation of the peopling of Polynesia becomes superfluous. For each little party of men and women who came to a new island bore within them the seed which would in course of time, with only a small rate of increase, populate not only that island, but all the others near it. As the population grew, other voyagers would be committed to the Pacific wastes, most to die, an occasional handful to carry their seed to a new island. Many voyagers would be men who had been carried away while fishing or making forays against neighbouring islands. The great events in the prehistory of the Pacific occurred when canoes with women aboard happened on previously uninhabited island groups.

Always it must be kept in mind what magic is effected by population increase while there is room to expand, and a sufficiency of food. The increase is slow at first, but faster as more people beget children in succeeding generations. In the light of this fact, the necessity of imagining shuttle services of Polynesian colonists in order to account for the populations disappears, just as it is unnecessary to think that the Polynesians brought canoe-loads of rats to the various groups in order to explain the presence of the millions of rats that flourished in historical times.

Numbers of Pacific ethnologists have traced the diffusion of artifacts from northern Europe, Asia and the East Indies to the Pacific Islands. One artifact which has taken a long time in arriving is Ockham's Razor. *Entia non sunt multiplicanda praeter necessitatem,* wrote William Ockham in the fourteenth century. This fundamental principle of logic and scientific method may be translated thus: 'Do not resort to elaborate explanations when simple ones will suffice.' It is unnecessary to think that Polynesian navigators, having noted their courses on outward voyages to distant islands which they did not know existed, sailed back by navigated voyages without instruments to their home islands, and then sailed to their distant discoveries on voyages of colonization. The view that the Polynesians settled their distant islands at the time they discovered them by unnavigated one-way voyages is both simple and realistic.

CHAPTER FIVE

THE VOYAGING TRADITIONS

THE view that Polynesian navigators, having discovered distant islands, sailed back to their home islands and then colonized their discoveries arose from European interpretations of Eastern Polynesian, Hawaiian, and New Zealand Maori voyaging traditions. The purpose of the present chapter is to show that these traditions embody transplanted and partially adapted traditional memories of Western Polynesian voyages in the Samoa-Tonga-Fiji area, and point to the Samoan island Savaii as the homeland of the Eastern Polynesian, Hawaiian, and New Zealand ancestors.

Throughout Eastern Polynesia, Hawaii, and New Zealand, 'Hawaiki' and its dialectal equivalents was an ancient traditional name for a homeland, to and from which the ancestors of the peoples of those islands were described in the traditions as voyaging.[1] Hawaiki was certainly a pre-European traditional name, having been recorded in the Tahitian islands as well as New Zealand at the time of Cook's first visit, and embodied in the name of the Hawaiian Islands.[2] The Eastern Polynesian name Hawaiki is the linguistic equivalent of the name of the main Samoan island, Savaii. The Samoan 's' is pronounced lightly and there is a check before the final vowel of Savaii.

Pursuing the name Hawaiki, we find that, according to information obtained from Tupaea and other Tahitians by Cook and his associates in 1769, an island with the equivalent name lay close to islands with names corresponding to those of Upolu and Tutuila, which are the other chief Samoan islands close to Savaii. These three islands were described as lying to the west. Tupaea showed them in a map which he drew for Cook, and described the island corresponding to Savaii as the 'father of all the islands'.[3]

A. S. Thomson, in his book *The Story of New Zealand*, published in 1859, cited a New Zealand Maori tradition, told to Sir George Grey some years previously, that 'Waerota, Rarotonga, Waeroti, Parima and Manono are islands near Hawaiki'. The Maoris had recited these names mechanically and with no knowledge of the geographical positions of the islands. Since 'Parima' and 'Manono' corresponded to Apolima and Manono, situated across Apolima Strait from the east coast of Savaii, Thomson conjectured that the Maori ancestors came from there, but made the mistake of thinking that they had come directly to New Zealand.[4] These names link up with the indications of Eastern Polynesian memories of the Samoan Savaii as the ancestral homeland.

Other New Zealand traditions which have puzzled anthropologists were collected in the late nineteenth century by the New Zealand prehistorian S. Percy Smith. These traditions had been dictated by the Maori priest Te Matorohanga and other older Maoris, and were published by Smith with a running commentary. According to these traditions, the main Maori colonists of New Zealand had been led by Toi, and had been preceded by dark people associated with the name Tau. Their voyages were associated with the place-names Hawaiki and Rarotonga. The Maoris did not know where these places were. Smith's conjecture was that the early dark people were probably not unlike the Moriori of the Chatham Islands; Elsdon Best called them Maruiwi after the name of a leader in the tradition; and both Smith and Best pictured these people as having migrated to New Zealand from the Melanesian area, thereby fixing the idea in the minds of most New Zealanders that dark 'Morioris' preceded the Polynesian settlers of New Zealand.[5]

Again the traditional names Hawaiki and Tau correspond to Samoan place-names: Savaii, the big Samoan island, and Tau.

Tau is the main island of Manua, the outlying Samoan group. Presumably in ancient times the Samoans of the other islands had a tradition of early dark people who had lived in Tau before the main Samoan stock arrived. The widespread Eastern Polynesian tradition of the Manahune, who were regarded as different from or inferior to the Polynesian aristocracy, may also be traced to this source.[6]

According to Maori traditions collected in the middle of the nineteenth century by Sir George Grey, Kupe and Ngahue were explorers who came from Hawaiki to New Zealand and returned to Hawaiki, whence colonists following Kupe's sailing directions came to New Zealand.[7] Later European reconstructionists, of whom Smith and Best were the chief, calculated that the main body of Maori tribal ancestors had arrived in the twelfth and fourteenth centuries, because the count-back of generations in the chiefly genealogies, calculated at twenty-five years to a generation, established those dates. The two principal migrations which were reconstructed by these methods were those of Toi and the 'Fleet'. These reconstructions were accepted as the broad prehistory of the Maori migrations to New Zealand.[8] Comparisons of Polynesian folk-lore made in the next six paragraphs, however, show that the story of Kupe's and Ngahue's discovery of New Zealand and return to Hawaiki with the news embodies an adapted Eastern Polynesian folk-tale based on Western Polynesian myths.

In the version of the Kupe story given to Grey, the three following incidents are mentioned. Kupe, after returning to Hawaiki from New Zealand, told the colonists who set out for New Zealand to 'keep ever steering to the eastward, where the sun rises'. (Later improvers changed Kupe's sailing directions to the south-west, thus fitting a Polynesian starting point.)[9] Kupe had left his brother Hoturapa to die before setting out for New Zealand. One of the labours of Kupe in New Zealand was to make openings in the land as signs that he had been there.

Mangarevan tradition has a similar story, in which Tupa commanded the first organized expedition to come to the island, arriving with his wife Naho after killing his brother Noe. Noe had been put on a raft which floated to Mangareva and cut a channel through the land.[10]

Tupa was also remembered in the Marquesas Group as a demigod with special associations with Havaii, and with the coast of Nuku Hiva near Ha'atuatua Bay, where, as Kupe did in the New Zealand version of the story, he changed the face of the countryside. Here his sister Hina said to him, 'Tupa, o atea' (Tupa, here comes the day). Haka Hotu was the chief of an island visited by Tupa.[11]

Hotu turned up in Easter Island as Hotu-matua, the founding father, after having fallen out with his brother who, like Kupe in the New Zealand story, was not above stealing a rival's bride.[12]

All these tales are variants of the Maui myths, which are widespread both in Western and Eastern Polynesia. In some variants Maui kills his sister Hina-uri's husband Ira-waru. In the Easter Island story Te Ira was Hotu's brother's rival whose bride was stolen. The names Kupe, Tupa, Rupe, Tu, Ru, Hotu, Maui, Maui-mua, Hina-uri, Hina-ika, Ngahue, Ngake and Naho were interchanged in the folk-lore of the various groups, including Tahiti and Rarotonga.[13]

It is interesting to see how the Kupe story was adapted in its various locales. In Marquesan tradition Tupa lands at Havaii, Fitinui, and an island in the Marquesas Group. In Mangareva Tupa comes from Havaiki to Mangareva and then goes to Hiva. In Easter Island Hotu-matua goes to his new home after being told of its existence through a soothsayer's dream, and stays there. In New Zealand Kupe comes from Hawaiki and then returns there, and later colonists follow his directions to New Zealand and thereafter revisit Hawaiki. Kupe even gets to the Chathams, where, like Kupe, Tupa and Maui elsewhere, he changes the local topography.[14]

These comparisons show that the folk-tales which have been used by Europeans for reconstructions of supposed Polynesian voyages to and from far places are myths.

The New Zealand Maoris, in accepting these tales as history, have gone farther than some of their ancestors, as the following quotation will show. In 1868, when the European rendering of Maori legend into alleged history was well under way, William Colenso, one of the few early Europeans who had lived among the old-time Maoris, commented:

> The names of several canoes are given, also of their crews and leaders; their marvellous adventures by the way; the numerous things they brought to New Zealand; and the height of the men, '9 and 11 feet'. Also, that some of them had previously discovered New Zealand, in a voyage of exploration purposely made hither, and having coasted and visited different parts of it, had returned to the mother country and had been the means of others coming to New Zealand to settle; and that many of the canoes, on reaching the land of New Zealand, immediately set about circumnavigating the Northern Island, &c., &c. In all this mythical rhapsody there is scarcely a grain of truth; and yet some educated Europeans have wholly believed it. The New Zealanders themselves never did so.[15]

When Cook visited New Zealand in 1769, some Maoris in the north of the North Island said that some of their people had visited a land to the N.W. by N. or N.N.W. where there were pigs. Tupaea, the Tahitian who accompanied Cook, told the Maoris they were liars, since the people in question had not brought any pigs back with them.[16] There is, however, no need to look for a land with pigs to the N.W. by N. or N.N.W. of New Zealand in vindication of the claim made by the Maoris to Tupaea. It can be explained as a variant of the Eastern Polynesian tradition of Hawaiki, placed vaguely in a westing direction, without adaptation of that direction to New Zealand, in accordance with the fact that voyagers in the days before instruments could not judge longitudes accurately.

The tradition of Hawaiki was not devoid of historical truth. All the peoples who came from Western Polynesia to Eastern Polynesia and thence to New Zealand and other peripheral islands brought with them their memories of Hawaiki, their former Western Polynesian homeland.

In view of the evidence pointing to Savaii as the vaguely remembered traditional homeland of the Eastern Polynesians, Hawaiians, and New Zealand Maoris, one might expect to find that traditional memories of Tonga, as well as Samoa, persisted in the voyaging traditions of those peoples. In this section evidence that it did will be given.

Vavau is the nearest of the main Tongan islands to Savaii, and there was two-way contact between them in early historical times (see Chapter One). An ancient and general traditional place-name in Eastern Polynesia and New Zealand was 'Wawau' and other dialectal equivalents of Vavau.[17] In the list of islands given by Tupaea to Cook and his associates in 1769 Vavau figures as the name of an island to the west; other names in the list—also for islands to the west—are 'Oweha' and 'Orotuma', which recall the western islands Uiha, Uvea, Lotuma, and Rotuma. David Porter, who visited Nuku Hiva in the Marquesas Group in 1813, was told that when the group was first peopled by 'Oataia, or daylight, and Ananoona, his wife', many plants had been brought from 'Vavao'.[18]

Another widespread traditional Eastern Polynesian name is Rarotonga and its dialectal equivalents; again this name occurs in New Zealand tradition. We have seen earlier in this chapter that according to a New Zealand tradition 'Waerota, Rarotonga, Waeroti, Parima and Manono are islands near Hawaiki', and that in another New Zealand tradition, the voyages of Maori colonists were associated with 'Hawaiki and Rarotonga'. In the New Zealand tradition of the colonization of New Zealand told to Sir George Grey, Rarotonga is described as being 'on the other side of Hawaiki'.[19] The equivalent of the name Raro-

These artifacts were acquired on Cook's first voyage, during which he visited the Tahitian islands and New Zealand. They comprise a tanged adze and its detached head, three instruments for puncturing the skin in tattooing, each viewed in two positions, and a mallet for striking these instruments. The tanging or reduction of the butt of the adze head as an aid in lashing it to the handle, which was typical of many Eastern Polynesian, Hawaiian, and New Zealand adzes, can be seen.

tonga appears in the list of island names given by Tupaea in 1769, and the old name for the modern Rarotonga (Tumu-te-varovaro) is given as that of a separate island. In a Mangarevan legend some early chiefs are described as sailing to and from Rarotonga.[20] The equivalent of the name Rarotonga occurs in Marquesan legend.[21] The inhabitants of Manihiki and Raka-hanga and Tongareva in the Northern Cooks had traditions that their ancestors came from Rarotonga.[22]

Vavau and the islands near it are 'near Hawaiki', and are 'on the other side of Hawaiki' in relation to Eastern Polynesia or to the east coast of Savaii, according with the view that the name Rarotonga originally referred to Tonga in relation to Savaii.

Since vestigial memories of Samoa and Tonga persisted in Eastern Polynesian, Hawaiian, and New Zealand voyaging traditions, it is not surprising that traces of a previous knowledge of Fiji did also. This does not necessarily mean that the Polynesians had come from Fiji. We have seen in Chapter One that the Tongans were in touch with Fiji in historical times, and the Western Polynesian ancestors of the Eastern Polynesians could have known of Fiji from similar contacts.

The main island of Fiji is Viti. Equivalents of this name, such as Fitinui, Tefiti, and Tawhiti, occur in Eastern Polynesian and New Zealand tradition, and the name Tahiti could also be an equivalent.[23] We have seen earlier in this chapter that in Marquesan tradition Tupa landed at both Fitinui and Havaii.

Abraham Fornander, who lived in the Hawaiian Islands for many years in the middle of the nineteenth century, noted that a place to and from which the Hawaiian ancestors sailed in legend was 'Katiki'—the Hawaiian equivalent of 'Tahiti'. Fornander tried to decide when the 'Katiki' referred to in the Hawaiian traditions meant the Tahiti of Eastern Polynesia or other far places in Polynesia, and when it meant a Tahiti outside Polynesia. He obtained on two islands identical versions of a prayer and chant about Kualii—a name which means Tu the

F

Chief. In this poem Kualii was described as visiting a country
with a different language, not inhabited by people like the
Hawaiians, but by 'haole', a word meaning people of white
skin, or foreigners.[24] Fornander commented that the reference
to the different language made this Tahiti unique in Hawaiian
tradition. This reference could well be a vestige of a tradition
of Viti, the mention of the differences from the Hawaiians being
a subsequent addition. Neither Fornander nor, apparently, his
Hawaiian informants connected the reference with Viti, making
it reasonable to think that, if it does refer to Viti, it had come
down from pre-European times.

It was suggested in Chapter One that 'Oheteroa', for which
Tupaea was looking when Cook encountered Rurutu, and
'Mannua', another island which Tupaea thought was in the
vicinity of 'Oheteroa', betokened traditional knowledge of Viti
in the Fiji Group and the Manua Group of Samoa. 'Hete' is
another equivalent of 'Hiti' or 'Viti', and 'roa' means 'long' or
'big'. Tupaea's list of islands, as we have seen earlier in the
present chapter, also contained the equivalent of the name of
Savaii, described as the 'father of all the islands', and of Upolu,
Tutuila, and Vavau. It might be expected, therefore, that Tupaea
would have had a vague traditional knowledge of Viti and
Manua also, without knowing the precise locations of these
places. 'Mannua' was described as an abode of cannibals and
spirits, linking up with the tradition of the Manahune referred
to earlier. Tupaea also stated that there were a number of
'Ohetes' in the neighbourhood of Rurutu, which accords with
the view that he had a vague knowledge of the Fiji Group.[25]
If Tupaea had visited Rurutu before he saw it from Cook's ship,
as he claimed, one wonders why he gave Cook the name of
Rurutu as that of a separate island from Oheteroa. Tupaea had
a motive for representing that he had direct knowledge of
traditionally known islands, since he was anxious to be taken
on the *Endeavour* when it left Tahiti.

The names Pukapuka and Rangiatea are other Eastern Polynesian place-names which are reminiscent of Western Polynesia.
Pukapuka is the name of an island in the Tuamotus and of
another in the Northern Cooks. It recalls the name of Puapua, a
place on the east coast of Savaii. The name of the Tahitian
island Borabora is probably a variant. Rangiatea was widespread
in Eastern Polynesia and New Zealand as a local place-name and
that of a traditional place.[26] Raiatea, the name of a Tahitian
island near Borabora, is an equivalent. The name Rangiatea
reputedly occurs in the *rongorongo* tablets of Easter Island,
which contain a form of writing.[27] Since Atea was the name of
a god in Eastern Polynesia, and the Marquesans, as we have
seen earlier in this chapter, had a tradition that Atea had come
from 'Vavao' as their founding ancestor, it is reasonable to think
that Rangiatea, meaning 'Heaven of Atea', was originally an
Eastern Polynesian name for the Western Polynesian home of
Atea.

So far we have confined our attention to traditional evidence
which was either gathered at the time of European contact, or
which contained or was accompanied by evidence making it
reasonable to believe that it had come down from pre-European
times. In this section we shall review some place-names in Eastern Polynesian voyaging traditions which have been repeatedly
cited as evidence of alleged prehistoric contacts over long distances, but which, when viewed in relation to an Eastern Polynesian provenance from Savaii, acquire a new significance.

In a chant declaimed in the year 1817 to a European missionary by two Tahitians, 'Havai'i' was referred to as 'birth-place
of lands', while 'Aihi' was described as being 'toward the
declining sun', where a mountain from which angry flames came
forth formed a boundary and landmark, and beyond which was
a place named 'Oahu'.[28] The conventional identification of
'Havai'i' has been with Raiatea in the Tahitian islands, but since

the description of 'Havai'i' as 'birth-place of lands' accords with
the Tahitian Tupaea's description of Savaii in Samoa as 'father
of all the islands', and with the other evidence of the tradition
of Savaii as the traditional Eastern Polynesian homeland, the
identification with Raiatea by the interpreters was somewhat
parochial. The conventional identification of Aihi, its flaming
mountain, and Oahu has been with Hawaii, Mauna Loa, and
Oahu, in the Hawaiian Islands. Aihi, however, was 'toward the
declining sun', which does not accord with the bearing of
Hawaii in relation to the Tahitian islands.

Further light on the flaming or raging mountain in the Hawaii
of Eastern Polynesian legend is given by Fornander's notes on
Marquesan voyaging traditions. In these traditions Hawaii was
one of the places on the migration route of Atea to the Marquesas Group. Fornander commented: 'Hawaii appears to have
been subject to tremendous hurricanes, followed by famines.
. . . Two mountains are mentioned in Hawaii; one in the mele
(song) of Matahou of Hawaii, called Mouna-Tika-oe; the other
in the mele of Tupaa, called Mauna-oa. The latter is said to
have been raging (ii) on top and served as a landmark for
Tupaa when he left Hawaii with his family and followers.'[29]

Since Atea, in the Marquesan legend recorded by Porter,
came from 'Vavao', since Samoa is subject to hurricanes, and
since volcanoes are no less plentiful in Western Polynesia than
in the Hawaiian Islands, it is evident that the Tahitians, having
inherited a chant embodying memories of Western Polynesia,
made additions to it from their own geographical knowledge.
In another version of the Tahitian chant, Ru is mentioned along
with Hina and Maui;[30] Tupaa is in the Marquesan variant.
There is a Maugaloa in Savaii, but since Maugaloa, Mauna-oa,
and Mauna Loa merely mean 'Long Hill', the name does not
provide a basis for a firm identification.

The Marquesan songs referring to Tupaa and Matahou give
further evidence that the Tupa of Marquesan tradition and the
Kupe of New Zealand Maori tradition stemmed from the same

legendary source, since the name of Kupe's canoe was Mata-hou-rua.[31]

The view that the Hawaiki of New Zealand and Cook Islands tradition was the Tahitian island of Raiatea stems from the identification of the 'Havai'i' of Tahitian legend with Raiatea. There is no evidence that Havai'i was a pre-European name for Raiatea.

In the same Tahitian chant which contained the reference to Havai'i as the birth-place of lands there is a reference to 'Nuuhiva', its direction being given as *toerau*. The conventional identification of Nuuhiva has been with Nuku Hiva in the Marquesas Group, about 1,000 miles north-east of the Tahitian islands. Since the equivalent of the name also occurs in the list of islands given to Cook by Tupaea, who placed it in an easting direction from Tahiti, it can be accepted that the Tahitians had pre-European knowledge of the Marquesas Group. A simple explanation of this knowledge is that some of the ancestors of the Tahitians came by one-way voyages to the Tahitian islands from the Marquesas Group. Evidence pointing to such a conclusion is reviewed in the last chapter of the present book. The view that Marquesans occasionally came to the Tahitian islands by one-way voyages is further supported by the fact that the winds south of the Marquesas Group prevail from the east. 'Nuku Hiva', however, merely means 'fleet of Hiva', Hiva being the basic place-name. For the following reasons it is uncertain whether references to 'Hiva' in Polynesian voyaging traditions are to islands in the Marquesas Group. The meaning of *toerau* and its dialectal equivalents in various Polynesian groups ranges from 'north-west' to 'north-east'.[32] It is unnecessary, therefore, to select from this wide range of interpretations the direction which suited Nuku Hiva rather than the east coast of Savaii. In a Rarotongan voyaging tradition, the name Iva is associated with the island Nukutere.[33] The name Iva recalls that of a village on the east coast of Savaii, from which the island of Apolima can be seen at a distance of a few miles. Nuu-tele, which is the Samoan

equivalent of the Rarotongan name Nukutere, is the name of
the main islet of Apolima. We have seen earlier in this chapter
that in Mangarevan folk-lore a demigod named Tupa was repre-
sented as sailing from Havaiki via Mangareva to Hiva.

When, therefore, Robert C. Suggs concluded that records of
deliberate voyages to and from the Marquesas Islands are
numerous in chants of Tahiti and Hawaii, and in legends of
Mangareva,[34] his implicit assumption that 'Hiva' in the folk-lore
of those islands necessarily referred to the Marquesas Group
was unjustified.

The geographical knowledge of the Polynesians has been repeatedly cited as evidence of former extensive two-way voyaging.[35] But, as we have seen, their pre-European knowledge of
distant islands is simply explained by the view that early settlers
or later migrants, coming from those islands by one-way voyages,
brought with them traditions of their homelands. Numbers of
European children born in Australia and the Pacific Islands
from 1800 onward have similarly known of the existence and
broad geography of distant lands from their forebears and other
migrants who came from those countries by one-way voyages.

In the later decades of the nineteenth century, numbers of
Europeans collected alleged evidence of former voyaging from
informants in the Pacific Islands. But by that time it was too
late to secure evidence that could reasonably be assumed to
throw light on voyaging in the pre-European period. From the
time of Cook onward, the Polynesians had learned of distant
islands from European explorers and missionaries and from
members of their own race who sailed round the Pacific in
European ships. It was inevitable that the Polynesian story-tellers
should have incorporated tales of former voyages to those islands
in their traditions. The Europeans in their traditions did much
the same. The only traditional evidence which can be taken as
applying to the pre-European period is that recorded at the
time of European contact or supported by evidence showing

that it is reasonably free of indirectly derived knowledge acquired in the post-European period.

In this section, some notable examples of overstatements by Europeans, based on late information about alleged former voyaging, will be reviewed.

In the years 1773 and 1774, a Tahitian named Hitihiti accompanied Cook to Tongatabu, New Zealand, and the Marquesas Group.[36] The Spaniard Andia, who visited Tahiti a few months after Hitihiti's return, was given lists of islands including the names 'Tonetapu', 'Iaotea', and 'Guaytaho', corresponding to Tongatabu, Aotea—a New Zealand Maori name for part of the North Island—and Vaitahu Bay in the Marquesan islands.[37] The name Aotea was thus added to the store of traditional names as the result of Cook's voyage. Earlier in the present chapter the Tahitian chant referring to Aihi, recorded in 1817, was considered. A variant of this chant, containing additional names of distant Polynesian islands, later came into the hands of S. Percy Smith. Among these added names was 'Aotea-roa o te Maori' (Aotea-roa of the Maori). Dismissing the explanation that this variant of the chant contained knowledge derived after the time of European contact, Smith suggested that the name Aotea-roa in it betokened prehistoric Tahitian knowledge of New Zealand.[38]

A late Rarotongan tradition said that Tangiia visited Rapanui (Easter Island) thousands of miles away, but an ethnologist has shown that there was no indigenous name for Easter Island,[39] Rapanui being a late invention by visiting sailors.

J. B. Stair, an early missionary in Samoa, recorded many pages of late traditions from a Rarotongan migrant to Samoa, who knew the geography of the Pacific well enough to take the early Rarotongans on voyages to every part of it.[40] Rarotonga became the happy hunting ground of European myth-makers. One of Smith's Rarotongan informants said he had been told as a boy that the New Zealand colonizing fleet had sailed from Rarotonga, and that one of the canoes had called in on the way back to Hawaiki.[41] He also remembered having been told that some preserved moa had been brought back from New Zealand by an explorer who preceded the fleet, and he added circumstantial details recapitulating Maori traditions about the doings of the explorer and the fleet. (But he did not remember a canoe named by Smith—a plain proof that Smith asked leading questions.) According to Smith the fact that the informant knew 'Aotearoa' as the name of New Zealand showed that the destination of the fleet was New Zealand. But Bishop Williams, who had lived among the New Zealand Maoris for many years, commented that the word 'Aotearoa' had no meaning for some older Maoris, and that Smith's translation, 'Long White Cloud', would not have been rendered in Maori as 'Aotearoa'.[42] No hint of these Rarotongan traditions was recorded by John Williams or other early missionaries in Rarotonga, although Williams himself visited New Zealand and lent a willing ear to other Rarotongan traditions.[43] Previous searchers who knew the Maori traditions had visited Rarotonga before Smith, and seventy-five years of frequent contact between Rarotonga and New Zealand had preceded their inquiries. These late traditions, therefore, cannot be regarded as free from post-European knowledge of New Zealand traditions, or from the influence of Smith's own view that the ancestors of the New Zealand Maoris sailed to New Zealand from Rarotonga. By the time Smith and his followers had finished their researches, they had taken prehistoric Polynesian navigators on visits as far afield as New Guinea and the Antarctic.

The gathering of alleged evidence of former voyaging from informants in the islands has been continued by various anthropologists into recent times. In Uvea, a detached atoll in the Western Polynesian area, E. G. Burrows, an American anthropologist, during the thirties of the present century, accepted as authentic history a story that in prehistoric times some male Uveans set out for and settled Uea in the Loyalty Islands, about 1,000 miles to the south-west of Uvea.[44] Since both Uvea and the

Loyalty Islands had long been French possessions, Uea had long been recognized as a Polynesian outlier, and the resemblance of the names Uvea and Uea is eye-catching, one need go no farther than the teachings of early French missionaries for a foundation for these late traditions.

The danger of assuming that the Polynesians were incapable of embodying European information and views in their own traditions is shown by the fact that Maretu, an educated Rarotongan who had been born before the early missionaries established themselves in Rarotonga, put forward the view that the Rarotongans had come from Eromanga in the New Hebrides.[45] Since the father of the Rarotongan mission, John Williams, was killed in Eromanga, and William Wyatt Gill, a close associate of Maretu in missionary work, thought the Polynesians came from Melanesia,[46] it cannot be accepted that Maretu's tradition was a pre-European one.

During the nineteen-thirties also, E. and P. Beaglehole, two New Zealand anthropologists, collected in Pukapuka, the westernmost atoll of the Northern Cooks, traditions of journeys to and from Niue and other islands by bearings on stars, and concluded that these stories embodied memories of former voyages by Pukapukans.[47] A visit to Niue from Pukapuka involves some 1,200 miles of southing and northing through waters beset by seasonally varying transverse currents. Bearings give no clue to lateral displacement by currents on such courses. Pukapuka and Niue are both small, isolated islands without peaks. No hint of how the course was determined in the first place was gleaned from the informants.

In a book published in 1961, Donald Marshall, an American anthropologist, tells of his visit to Raivavae, an isolated island on the southern fringe of Eastern Polynesia. Marshall, who accepted alleged traditions of former voyaging by Raivavans to New Zealand and Hawaii and back, gathered in Raivavae earlier in the twentieth century by J. F. Stimson, asked an informant in Raivavae whether the navigators had sailed by the stars; he received the answer that the informant had no knowledge of the methods of navigation used in former times.[48] Marshall did not himself offer any views on how the navigators on their outward journeys to New Zealand and Hawaii could have known when they had reached their latitudes, or whether they were east or west of their objectives, or how they could have determined the same details on the homeward journeys to their small island.

Anthropologists and historians who place credence in late traditions of former long voyaging overlook the fact that the parents or grandparents or great-grandparents of their informants could have used indirect geographical knowledge in these traditions, as a modern writer of historical novels frequently does in his stories.

All maritime peoples, particularly those living near great oceans, possessed folk-lore of voyages to and from lands far across the sea. The Celts had their Avalon, the Arabs their Sindbad who visited the land of the Great Roc, the Greeks their Ulysses who came upon the island of Circe, the Peruvian Indians their Tupac Yupanqui who visited some islands in the Pacific, the Romans their Islands of the Blest beyond the Pillars of Hercules. The story-teller, who takes his environment for his material and thereby imparts a substratum of reality to his tale, must use his imagination if he is to achieve the quality of romance. The Polynesians were one of the most poetic of people. Why is their folk-lore singled out for the dreary process of reduction to an unconvincing realism?

Here is a Polynesian travel tale which has its appeal and meaning, provided one does not edit all the life out of it in an attempt to represent it as history. It was collected by William Wyatt Gill on Aitutaki in the Southern Cooks, and is given in his English translation, in which he said he tried to preserve the archaic appeal of the original.[49] The reader will note that this Eastern Polynesian story has place-names suggesting Samoan and Fijian backgrounds.

In the fairy land of Kupolu there lived the renowned chief Rata, who resolved to build a great double canoe, with a view of exploring other lands. Shouldering his axe, he started off to a distant valley where the finest timber grew. Close to the mountain stream stood a fragrant tree, where a deadly combat was going on between a beautiful white heron and a spotted sea-serpent. . . . The beautiful bird was living but very much exhausted. Its unrelenting foe, sure of victory, was preparing for a final attack when Rata chopped it to pieces with his axe, and thus saved the life of the white heron. . . . From the branch of a distant tree the heron watched the labours of Rata throughout the livelong day. As soon as the chief had disappeared in the evening, the grateful bird started off to collect all the birds of Kupolu to hollow out Rata's canoe. They gladly obeyed the summons of their sovereign, and pecked away with their beaks until the huge logs were speedily hollowed out. . . . It was almost dawn ere the work was completed. Finally they resolved to convey the canoe to the beach close to Rata's dwelling. To accomplish this each bird took its place on either side of the canoe, completely surrounding it. At a given signal they all extended their wings, one to bear up the canoe, the other for flight. As they bore the canoe through the air they sang, each with a different note. . . . On reaching the sandy beach in front of the dwelling, the canoe was carefully deposited by the birds, who now quickly disappeared in the depths of the forest. . . .

Rata speedily provided his bird-built canoe with a mast and sail, and then summoned his friends, and laid in food and water for his projected voyage. Everything being now ready, he went on board. . . . The crafty Nganaoa, seeing the canoe start without him, ran to fetch an empty calabash, knocked off the top, and squeezing himself in as best he could, floated himself off on the surface of the ocean, until he got a little ahead of the canoe. . . . A voice now issued from the calabash. 'O Rata, take me on board your canoe!' 'Whither away?' inquired the chief. 'I go,' said the poor fellow inside the calabash, 'to the Land of Moonlight, to seek my parents. . . .' Rata now asked, 'What will you do for me if I take you in?' . . . [Nganaoa promised] to destroy all the monsters of the ocean which might infest their path. . . .

Swiftly and pleasantly, with a fair wind, they sped over the ocean in quest of new lands. One day Nganaoa shouted, 'O Rata, here is a terrible foe starting up from the main.' It was an open

clam of fearful proportions. . . . In a moment this horrid clam
might crush them all by suddenly closing its mouth. But Nganaoa
was ready. . . . He seized his long spear and quickly drove it
down into the fish. . . .

Again they pursued their voyage in safety. But one more great
peril awaited them. One day the brave Nganaoa shouted, 'O Rata,
here is a great whale!' The enormous mouth was wide open, one
jaw beneath the canoe and the other above it. The whale was evidently bent on swallowing them up alive. Nganaoa, the slayer
of monsters, now broke his long spear in two, and at the critical
moment, when the whale was about to crush them all, he cleverly
inserted both stakes inside the mouth of their foe, so that it became
impossible for it to close its jaws. Nganaoa nimbly jumped inside
the mouth of this great whale and looked down its stomach, and
lo! there sat his long lost father Tairitokerau and his mother
Vaiaroa, who had been swallowed alive when fishing by this
monster of the deep. [The monster swam to the nearest land,
where, on reaching the beach, father, mother and son walked out
through the open mouth of the whale.]

The island proved to be Iti-te-marama, or Moonlight. Here the
canoe of Rata was drawn up on the beach, and for a time they all
lived pleasantly. They daily refreshed themselves with its fruits
and fish, adorning their persons with fragrant flowers. At length
they longed for the land of their birth in Avaiki, and they resolved
to return. The canoe was prepared and launched. Food and water
were laid in. The great mat sail was set up, and at length the
brave navigator Rata, with the parents of Nganaoa and the entire
party, started once more. After many days, but without further
peril, they eventually reached their original homes in the lands
of the sun-setting.

The true traditionalists are those who wish to see the Polynesian traditions restored to their form before Europeans 'edited'
them.

CHAPTER SIX

MIGRANTS FROM THREE KINGDOMS

IN this chapter the relationship of prehistoric Polynesian voyaging to the distribution of Polynesian useful plants, livestock, and artifacts is discussed.

The introduced plants of Polynesia have been repeatedly cited as evidence of the deliberate colonization of distant islands. Purpose of course entered into their transfer insofar as exiles who had loaded up canoes with plants and other commodities, or people who had been blown away while carrying them between local islands, arrived on distant groups. It is, however, unnecessary to believe that, when new islands were discovered in prehistoric times, the discoverers found they had forgotten their useful plants and had to return home by deliberate navigation to get them.

The two plants which required most nurture on long voyages were the breadfruit and banana, because the usual method of propagation was from shoots and sprouts which needed tending. Their presence on remote groups such as Hawaii is evidence that they were placed deliberately in canoes and tended on journeys to those groups. But obviously the necessary care would have been given by one-way voyagers who hoped to establish these plants in new settlements. When, therefore, Peter Buck invoked the presence of the breadfruit and banana on distant Polynesian islands as evidence of planned settlement,[1] he proved his point that voyages of fishermen and others who had not made systematic preparations could not account for the transfer of these plants, but fell far short of proving that the discoverer-settlers of Hawaii and other distant groups did not bring breadfruit and banana plants with them but introduced them by subsequent voyages to and from their home islands.

The taro and sweet potato, which were usually propagated from parts of tubers, were suitable for carriage on long voyages. The coconut provided food and drink on such voyages; it strikes easily when planted out on warm strands. The yam and sugar-cane were two other useful plants suited to transfer, being propagable from those parts of the plant which are used for food. The great majority of introduced useful plants found on the farther Polynesian islands could be grown from seeds occupying little space.

The botanical facts, then, are certainly compatible with one-way transfer by discoverer-settlers; in addition, it is reasonable to believe that one-way voyagers would have been particularly careful to preserve their plants, in order to provide for their needs when they found new land. Moreover, if the early settlers of Polynesia plied back and forth between distant islands fetching plants, some strange omissions occurred. For example, according to George Turner the sweet potato was not established in Samoa until European times.[2] The *fe'i* banana, which formed the main food reserve in Tahiti, is also considered to have been of post-European introduction in Hawaii, where it does well in suitable locations.[3]

Another assumption which is unwarranted is that the plants of historical times in a particular island group all came from the same source. These plants need not have all arrived with the first continuing settlers of that group. Some might have come in later canoes from different islands. It is also possible that on occasion plants were brought by migrants who arrived before the first party of continuing settlers but did not leave descendants. In the case of the sweet potato, there is evidence, reviewed in the last chapter of this book, that whereas most of the introduced Polynesian plants came from the west, this important Polynesian food plant came from America.

Pigs, dogs, fowls, and rats were present on various Polynesian islands at the time Europeans arrived. They were not indigenous in the Pacific Islands. Their presence can be accounted for in the same way as that of the introduced plants: by one-way transfer over the larger gaps between islands by exiles and people blown away while transporting them on local voyages. It is reasonable to believe that one-way voyagers would have been careful to preserve their livestock for breeding purposes. The Polynesians were well aware of the importance of these items to their economy.

The distribution of the pig, dog, and fowl in the Polynesian islands was irregular, as the notes given in the following three paragraphs show. While livestock could have died out after introduction to an island group, the evidence as a whole is difficult to reconcile with the thought that Polynesian voyagers sailed back and forth between distant islands in prehistoric times.

Pigs reached most parts of Polynesia. The high, fertile groups were ideal for them. At the time of early European contact they flourished in Samoa, Tahiti, Rarotonga, Atiu, the Marquesas Group, and Hawaii. All that was necessary to establish the pig was a boar and sow. Yet at the time of European discovery a number of Polynesian islands suited to the pig did not have it. Easter Island was one,[4] Niue another. When John Williams made contact with Niue and offered the islanders some cooked pork, they had no knowledge of this food and thought Williams was giving them human flesh.[5] This naturally perturbed them, because they thought he might want to replenish his supplies at their expense! If the pig had ever arrived on Easter Island or Niue in prehistoric times, it had died out, and the people of Niue did not even have any tradition of it. Because these two islands are isolated, it is reasonable to suspect that the pig had never been established on them. The fowl, on the other hand, had got to Easter Island and had been preserved into post-European times. Other Polynesian islands which lacked the pig were Mangaia and Aitutaki, although there were pigs within 100 miles of them on Rarotonga and Atiu.[6] Aitutaki, however, had the fowl.[7] Since the fowl was easily transportable by breeding stock or by a hen on eggs, its presence on distant islands is not evidence of two-way contact with those islands.

The Polynesian dog was well adapted to surviving long voyages also. He even reached New Zealand and Hawaii. Again, therefore, his widespread distribution in Polynesia is not evidence of two-way contacts over long distances in prehistoric times. On the other hand some caution is necessary in attaching significance to the dog's absence from various islands in historical times. Sometimes he was considered more of a nuisance than he was worth. Mariner tells of a chief of one of the Tongan islands who had all the dogs destroyed for this reason.[8] Dogs, moreover, were competitors with man for animal food, and were themselves a source of food for man, making them likely to be casualties in time of famine.

New Zealand had the dog, but not the pig or fowl. Again, however, it is doubtful whether this is significant of anything more than that the pig and fowl may not have been hardy enough to survive voyages to New Zealand in prehistoric times. Thus when Cook took some Polynesian pigs and fowls on his vessel on his first visit to New Zealand, they proved susceptible to the cold and died before the ship arrived there.[9]

The rat was ubiquitous in Polynesia, but this is not evidence of two-way contacts over long distances. The rat was well adapted for transfer either as a source of food or as a stowaway, and multiplied rapidly where the food supply was good. When John Williams came to Rarotonga there was a plague of rats.[10]

George Vason's evidence of the carrying capacity of one large double canoe, cited in Chapter Four, merits repetition here, since it refutes any suggestion that a small party of random voyagers in one canoe could not have brought with them many Polynesian livestock items, useful plants, and other commodities: 'Vason accompanied over 250 armed Tongan warriors in one double canoe at the end of the eighteenth century. This human cargo represents a weight of about twenty tons, which is equiva-

Albion Wright

Moa-hunter buried with adzes, whale teeth and moa egg, reconstructed with actual grave materials by Canterbury Museum, Christchurch, New Zealand.

lent to that of thirty persons, two boars, three sows, twelve piglets, thirty fowls, ten dogs, twenty rats, a hundred balled or
potted breadfruit and banana plants, and twelve tons of water-
gourds, seeds, yams, tubers, coconuts, adzes and weapons. A
double canoe one-third the size would have been ample for
viable settlement.' Nevertheless there is no conclusive evidence
that either the animals or plants found in historical times in any
island group all arrived there with the first continuing settlers.
Some may have come after or before these settlers. The pig,
dog, fowl, and rat need not always have arrived on distant islands
in company with human beings. Canoes which were left at the
water's edge were frequently borne away in storms. Polynesian
canoes were no doubt much like those of fishing people elsewhere, with fish offal and trash below decks, and pigs, dogs,
fowls, and rats wandering round. Canoes which were swept
away in storms with livestock only could occasionally have
arrived on remote islands during the several thousand years
of the Polynesian dispersal. It is also possible that human
beings died of exposure on long voyages, leaving their canoes
to livestock. Animals could have been kept alive on rainwater
in the bottoms of canoes.

Plants and livestock were not the only things which were
taken to distant islands by prehistoric Polynesian voyagers.
Adzes and other artifacts, and the techniques for making them,
were also conveyed far afield. The relationship of their diffusion
to the nature of prehistoric Polynesian voyaging is a matter of
considerable interest, as the notes given in this section will
show.

In 1939 R. Piddington quoted with approval a suggestion
made by E. S. C. Handy in 1930 that the cultures of Polynesia
could best be explained by the view that sporadic accidental
movements took place over several millennia.[11] Handy had not
developed his suggestion in detail. He also conceded that the
Maori migrations to New Zealand might have been excep-

tional. Piddington supported Handy's generalization by citing William Wyatt Gill's accounts of accidental voyages, from west to east and from east to west (see Chapter Four). In 1957 W. H. Goodenough pointed out that primary settlement by infrequent west-east voyages and secondary settlement by more frequent east-west voyages with the prevailing winds and currents yielded fruitful explanations of linguistic and cultural distributions in the Pacific Islands.[12] It is in accord with the relative unsuitability of the summer westerlies for west-east voyages that few artifacts of Western Polynesian type have been found in Eastern Polynesia, apart from those unearthed by Robert C. Suggs at Ha'atuatua Bay in the Marquesas Group.[13] It is no less in accord with the expectation of more frequent westing settlement with the prevailing winds and currents after primary west-east settlement that the Cooks, New Zealand, and Hawaii all possessed adzes and other cultural features of Eastern Polynesian type.[14]

After the internal populations of the high, fertile groups of Polynesia had increased, later arrivals would have had comparatively little effect on the existing cultures, apart from introducing a new plant or livestock item. They might, however, have occasionally imported a novel type of artifact or other minor cultural innovation, without substantially changing the existing culture of an island group as it was at the time they arrived. On the low, detached atolls of Polynesia, however, as A. P. Vayda, an American anthropologist, has pointed out, later handfuls of migrants could have had a relatively greater impact on the existing cultures, being more numerous in proportion to the existing populations of these atolls.[15]

Roger Duff, a New Zealand anthropologist who has made a special study of adze distributions, claiming that no adzes with butts tanged as an aid in lashing the handles have been established for Western Polynesia, whereas tanged adzes have been found throughout Eastern Polynesia, has argued that this is not in accord with what one would expect from random voyaging.[16] At the time of early European contact with Polynesia, however, random voyages from Eastern to Western Polynesia were still occurring (see Chapter Four). Obviously, therefore, there must have been some explanation for the absence of tanged adzes from Western Polynesia other than that random voyages did not occur. Apparently handfuls of migrants from Eastern Polynesia failed to establish the tanging of adzes among the conservative Western Polynesians.

Duff also argued that the existence of concentric rings of diffusion of distinctive adze types from the Tahitian islands to the other groups with Eastern Polynesian cultures is not in conformity with diffusion solely by random voyages. Suggs's evidence pointing to the Marquesas Group as an important early centre of diffusion in Eastern Polynesia,[17] however, introduces cross-ripples in Duff's concentric rings of diffusion. Nevertheless the Tahitian islands were no doubt an important centre of diffusion, since they are centrally placed for throwing off one-way migrants.

Tanged adzes have been found not only in Eastern Polynesia, but also in parts of East Asia and the East Indies. A number of archaeologists have concluded that the tanging of adzes was brought to Polynesia by migrants from the west, although tanging is not typical of Western Polynesian, Melanesian or Micronesian adzes.[18] If this were so, it would not follow that the founding settlers of Eastern Polynesia and Western Polynesia came separately to those areas from a common proto-Polynesian area, or that the Western Polynesians, before the Eastern Polynesians left Western Polynesia, practised the tanging of adzes. The facts could be explained by the view that, after the Eastern Polynesians left Western Polynesia, some random migrants who had by-passed Western Polynesia introduced the art of tanging into Eastern Polynesia. Perhaps the best view of all, however, is that after the early settlers of Eastern Polynesia were released from the conservative influence of Western Polynesian technology, they tanged some of their adzes and made other innovations in their artifacts.

Recent advances in Polynesian archaeology vindicate claims that archaeology can throw considerable light on cultural provenances. But the early distribution of plants, animals and artifacts as revealed by archaeological excavations cannot determine the scale or character of initial settlement of the various Pacific groups, since archaeology has no way of establishing beyond doubt the location or size of the site or sites of that settlement. Recent research into the distribution of blood factors in the Pacific populations, discussed in the last chapter of the present book, points to settlement by small, randomly selected parties.

CHAPTER SEVEN

THE LONELY ISLANDS

OUTSIDE the main groups of Polynesia lie a number of isolated islands that are full of lessons about the nature of prehistoric Polynesian voyaging and settlement.

Three islands lying north of the equator, Palmyra, Washington, and Fanning, unlike most of the other atolls in the mid-Pacific area, have a moderate rainfall and a substantial cover of vegetation in their middle areas.[1] They are also outside the main hurricane zone. Yet all three were uninhabited at the time of European discovery. On the other hand Tongareva, Manihiki, Rakahanga, and Pukapuka, lying several hundred miles to the south, were inhabited, although their rainfall is lighter and they are in the hurricane area.

It cannot be argued that Palmyra, Washington, and Fanning were uninhabited because they were off the track of the navigated voyages supposed to have been made in Polynesia in earlier times, for they are between Tahiti and Hawaii. Survival on the less arid islands outside the area of hurricanes should have been likelier, yet it was on the less desirable islands nearer to Tahiti that continuing colonies were found.

If one looks at these facts in relation to nautical realities, they fall in line with what one would expect. Fanning, Washington, and Palmyra are more or less in the path of the prevailing winds from the south-east, and are a long way from the central belt of Polynesian islands, whereas the inhabited atolls of the Northern Cooks are strung out from east to west and are much nearer the central belt. These inhabited atolls, therefore, were more likely to be reached by random voyagers.

A number of relics of former occupation found on Fanning have been discussed by the archaeologists K. P. Emory and B.

R. Finney. These relics included an enclosure of coral blocks marking the outlines of a rectangular building which, Emory and Finney considered, showed similarities to some Tongan structures, and basalt adzes which must have come from a high volcanic island, since basalt does not occur naturally on low atolls. These adzes resembled Tongan or Samoan types. No adzes made of the local tridacna shell, such as were used on most inhabited atolls, were found on Fanning. Also among the finds were fishhooks of indeterminate ancestry, but like Western Polynesian ones in some respects, and several raised graves containing human bones and the remains of ornaments made from drilled teeth of porpoise or whale.

Since the prevailing south-east winds blow from the Marquesas Group towards Fanning, the following reconstruction is suggested. A vessel with men only, or with men and women who did not leave descendants, came from the Marquesas Group at a time when its culture was more like that of its Western Polynesian provenance than in later days. (Archaeological excavations in the Marquesas Group by Robert C. Suggs have revealed evidence that the early culture of that group showed affinities with the cultures of Western Polynesia.)[2] The wanderers were lucky enough to come on Fanning. They had a few basalt adzes on board. These lasted them out, and they did not make others from the unfamiliar tridacna. In their strange new world they fashioned blocks out of coral and made a house. Rolling the blocks into position would not have required many workers. After a while the older people died. They were buried reverently, and the drilled ornaments which they had brought with them were buried in their graves. Finally, the last survivor died. The bones of the corpse which nobody remained to bury rotted away, but the tombs retained the bones of his companions.

Malden Island, another of the mid-Pacific atolls, although uninhabited at the time of European discovery, bore signs of early occupation over an appreciable period. Rubbish heaps and numerous structures and graves make it plain that at some time there must have been a continuing settlement including women. Nor is it difficult to conjecture why it disappeared. Little hollows for collecting water, some with the dippers still lying in them, were found all over the island, and the island itself is in the hurricane area. Thus too little water in time of drought, and other natural hazards, made life precarious. In some calamity the island became depopulated, and no other men and women arrived thereafter and left descendants.

On the chain of isolated and uninhabited mid-Pacific atolls stretching from Malden to Palmyra, then, we see impressive evidence of the hit-and-miss character of one-way voyaging. Palmyra does not appear to have been occupied, although it was a particularly desirable atoll if one had a choice. Christmas and Washington possessed a few relics of temporary occupation, and on Fanning a brief period of occupation can be traced. On Malden alone did a canoe with women aboard clearly establish a settlement which lasted for several generations.

The sparse signs of human occupation on these atolls, lying though they do between the central belt of Polynesian islands and Hawaii, give reason to believe that voyagers to Hawaii from the central belt, particularly including women, must have been rare.

There is great pathos about the signs of transient occupation on some of the uninhabited mid-Pacific atolls. Did some people who had set out from the Marquesas Group for delectable traditional islands strike one of them? If they did, it would have proved less than Paradise, being not fifteen feet above the sea, and offering little more than sea-food to live on. Perhaps the only inhabitants were fishermen who were driven to these atolls by storms.

We come now to the inhabited atolls of the Northern Cooks and Tokelaus,[3] a few hundred miles north of the central belt of Polynesian islands. The occupants of Tongareva, Manihiki, and Rakahanga, the easternmost of these atolls, had traditions that their ancestors had come from 'Rarotonga'. This name cannot be taken to refer to the modern Rarotonga. For reasons given in Chapter Five, this widespread Eastern Polynesian traditional name points to a vestigial memory of Tonga. The more obvious sources of settlement of the Northern Cooks are the Marquesas Group, the Tuamotus, and the Tahitian islands, whence come the prevailing winds and currents. The Northern Cooks have affinities in language and culture with the eastern groups of Polynesia; Pukapuka, the westernmost island, and the nearest to Western Polynesia, shows some intermixture of Western Polynesian elements. Williams's and Gill's accounts of accidental voyages from Rurutu to Manihiki and Fakaofo to Nassau (see Chapter Four) show that one-way settlers could have been borne to the Northern Cooks from both Eastern and Western Polynesia. The mixing of Eastern and Western Polynesian cultural elements in Pukapuka is in accord with A. P. Vayda's suggestion that later migrants to atolls with small populations might have had an appreciable impact on the existing cultures.

Moving west from Pukapuka, we come to the Tokelaus: Fakaofo, Nukunonu, and Atafu. When Horatio Hale visited the Tokelaus in 1841,[4] he recorded that the various islands of the group were in touch with one another over the short distances which separate them, but not with islands outside the group. Yet Hale also recorded that the people of the Tokelaus knew the place-name Pukapuka. Since Pukapuka lies immediately to the east, whence come the prevailing winds and currents, its name could have been brought to the Tokelaus by casual migrants, although Pukapuka and variants of this name—probably derived originally from Puapua, on the east coast of Savaii—were widespread in Eastern Polynesia. Since westerlies occasionally blow towards the east in the latitudes of the Tokelaus and Pukapuka, the Pukapukans could have known of the Tokelaus and Samoa from casual migrants from those islands.

It is in conformity with the Tokelaus' position in relation to the prevailing winds and currents from the south-east and east that Hale found that his Samoan interpreter could talk fairly easily with the people of the Tokelaus, and that there is evidence also of Eastern Polynesian influence in the group.

To complete our running survey of the atolls north of the central belt of Polynesian islands, let us consider the low atolls of the Phoenix Group. They were uninhabited at the time of European discovery, although there were signs of human occupation on some of them, as well as the inevitable rats.[5] Some of the Phoenix Islands are in a zone of appreciable rainfall. These islands have been used in modern times to relieve population pressure in the Gilbert Islands, which were much congested at the time of European contact.[6] Yet the Gilbert Islanders had not colonized them in prehistoric times, although they are only a few hundred miles to the east of the Gilberts. These facts are in conformity with the infrequency of west-east settlement. The west-setting equatorial current is particularly strong in the mid-Pacific area lying between the Gilberts and Tahiti, and the monsoonal winds which blow in the summer months from the north-west become more sporadic in this area. All these facts are difficult to reconcile with Peter Buck's view that voyagers from Micronesia sought out Tahiti over 2,000 miles to the south-east.[7]

South of the main Polynesian groups lie some more lonely outposts. They are high islands in areas where rainfall is reasonably adequate and cyclones are not devastating.

Easter Island, one of these outposts, 1,450 miles from the nearest other habitable land, had a flourishing colony when the Dutch voyager Roggeveen discovered it in 1722. The language of Easter Island is essentially Polynesian.[8] The traditional evidence reviewed in Chapter Five indicates that the Easter Islanders shared the general Eastern Polynesian traditional memories of Western Polynesia. Westerlies are a feature of the meteorology of the Easter Island area at a certain time of the year.[9] As de Bisschop proved on his raft voyage to the east (see

Chapter Three), east-setting currents also are occasionally encountered south of the central islands of Polynesia. It can be
concluded, therefore, that the original settlers of Easter Island
came from Polynesia. It is probable that Polynesian one-way
migrants were borne to Easter Island at varying times from both
the Marquesas Group and Mangareva. Some migrants from
Easter Island may have got to the main belt of Polynesian
islands, either by intent or accident, with the help of the prevailing winds and currents. If, however, any such incidents led
to attempts by Polynesians to sail deliberately for Easter Island,
it would have been a miracle if they had found it, since a direct
course with the unpredictable westerlies of the summer months
would have been difficult to sustain for 2,000 miles, and an
indirect course with the more sustained westerlies in latitudes
south of the central belt involves a sophisticated knowledge of
the meteorology which would be difficult to account for. It is
possible that, after the settlement of Easter Island from Polynesia, casual migrants from America occasionally arrived.[10]

A radiocarbon dating of human occupation by about 400
A.D. was obtained on Easter Island by Heyerdahl's expedition
to the island a few years ago.[11] Whether this occupation was by
transient or permanent occupants and whether the date will be
supported by other contemporaneous or closely succeeding dates
is not clear.

At the time of European contact the Easter Islanders had the
fowl, rat, banana, taro, sweet potato, sugar-cane, yam, and paper
mulberry, but not the pig or dog.[12] Later arrivals, either with or
without women, after continuing settlement had commenced,
might have introduced plants or livestock not already there.

Next we come to mysterious Pitcairn. This high, fertile
island is situated about 100 miles from a chain of deserted atolls.
The nearest land with any continuity of occupation is Mangareva, some 350 miles to the north. Pitcairn, however, is well

within striking distance of random voyagers from any of a host of islands to the north, west, and east of Mangareva.

When the *Bounty* mutineers arrived on Pitcairn, they broke up the ruins of structures left by previous occupants of the island. Many relics were buried beyond the newcomers' reach. Later archaeologists have described and discussed the remains.[13] There were three lots of stone structures, at least one of which was associated with burials. Among the material in the graves were bits of pearl shell which must have been imported to Pitcairn. There were also great numbers of adzes made from local stone. One type predominated, but there were others incorporating many different features of construction. The adzes bore resemblances to those of various inhabited Polynesian islands. The mutineers also found a number of breadfruit trees.

It has been supposed on the following traditional evidence that Pitcairn was deliberately colonized by Mangarevans who retained contact with their home island. The traditions of Mangareva collected by H. Laval, a nineteenth century missionary, contained references to Matakiterangi, a traditional island said to have been colonized by one of the early Mangarevan chiefs who planted breadfruit there.[14] This island was described as being 'like Petania', or 'in truth Petania'. Petania was the late Mangarevan name for Pitcairn, after both islands had been discovered by the British. When Laval's material was recorded for him by an educated Polynesian, Pitcairn was known to the Mangarevans from visits in European ships. Such evidence is not a valid basis for a theory that Pitcairn was colonized by Mangarevans.

The temporary character of the Polynesian occupation of Pitcairn has been considered a matter for which no firm explanation can be made. It becomes less puzzling if one thinks in terms of one-way migration rather than of Polynesian navigation at will. There are no signs on Pitcairn to show whether more than one lot of voyagers arrived there, but several separate parties might well have done so, in view of Pitcairn's nearness to so many Tuamotuan atolls. Whether the occupants of Pitcairn, like those of Malden, included women, is not clear.

Why should there have been a large number of differing adze types on Pitcairn, resembling types in distant islands? The early settlers of Pitcairn might have experimented with the local stone. This could also have happened in New Zealand, where a variety of archaic adze types has been found. Some of the resemblances between Pitcairn and New Zealand adze types may therefore be accidental.[15]

Rapa, the easternmost island of the Austral Group, some hundreds of miles south of the central belt of Polynesia, is another small, high island. Its culture is again essentially Polynesian. Heyerdahl's expedition unearthed extensive stone fortifications and house sites on its high ridges, with evidence of irrigation and intensive cultivation farther down.[16] It was, however, unnecessary for Heyerdahl to invoke the threat of attacking fleets from other islands to account for all this, since internal population increase and competition is a sufficient explanation.

Despite its isolation and smallness, Rapa was one of the minority of lonely islands at a distance from the central belt which had a continuing colony at the time of European contact. Yet Rapa did not retain all the migrants who came there against their will. It will be remembered from Chapter Four that a party of men and women were borne on a raft from Mangareva to Rapa, a distance of about 600 miles. They thought they had come from the south-east instead of the north-east. When they had rested and fitted out their raft, some of them, despite the hospitable attempts of the Rapans to dissuade them, waited for a following wind from the north-west and then pushed off to the south-east, where in fact no land lies before the polar ice is reached.[17] One can only guess at how many human ordeals ended in tragedy during the settlement of Polynesia.

Some distance west of Rapa lie the other islands of the Austral Group: Raivavae, Tubuai, Rurutu, and Rimatara.

Raivavae, Tubuai, and Rurutu are more or less in line with one another and with the direction of the prevailing wind from the south-east. This was not a favourable situation for deliberate voyaging in both directions between these islands, since on the leg towards the south-east the voyagers would have had to depend on the more capricious westerlies of the summer months. It is not surprising, therefore, that James Morrison, one of the mutineers of the *Bounty* which called at Tubuai in 1789, wrote of the inhabitants: 'They have no sailing vessels and never leave the land except they are blown off as all the islands of which they have any account are at too great a distance for them to hold any intercourse.'[18] Tubuai is situated between Rurutu and Raivavae at about 100 miles from each. Morrison's evidence gives a very different picture from that of Stimson's twentieth century informants on Raivavae, who described their ancestors as having sailed to New Zealand and Hawaii and back (see Chapter Five).

The names of Raivavae, Rurutu and Tubuai appear among the list of islands named by Tupaea the Tahitian at the time of Cook's visit to Tahiti in 1769.[19] This is compatible with the fact that one-way voyagers from these islands could fetch up in the Tahitian islands with the winds from the south-east and south. In John Williams's time a chief from Rurutu was carried to Raiatea in this way.[20] It is also possible that voyagers driven from the Tahitian islands or the Tuamotus to Rurutu or Tubuai or Raivavae managed to get to the Tahitian islands occasionally with the help of the trade wind. Trying to rediscover such small islands in the teeth of the prevailing wind or with the aid of the capricious westerlies would, of course, have been a different matter.

William Ellis recorded that people from Rimatara were on Rurutu at the time of European contact, and in due course got back to their own island about ninety miles away.[21] It is not clear whether the visit was deliberate, but both Rimatara and Rurutu are conveniently placed for sailing across the prevailing wind in both directions.

That a long ordeal occasionally ended happily is shown by the presence of the Polynesians on distant islands. A tale of chivalry and romance after such an ordeal was recorded by Moerenhout, an early visitor to Rimatara.[22] A Tahitian lady who had been converted to Christianity was the sole survivor of an accidental voyage to Rimatara, an isle which Moerenhout and others described as something of an earthly Paradise. She became the bride of a local chief, converted him, and inspired him to defeat his enemies!

Contact within the Southern Cooks, lying to the west of the Australs, was also apparently conditioned by the meteorology of the area.

It has been mentioned in Chapter Two that the chief of Atiu told John Williams how he sailed to Rarotonga about 116 miles to the south-west. The Atiuans were also in two-way contact with Mitiaro, about twenty miles north-east of Atiu, and Mauke, about a similar distance south-east of Mauke.[23] Two-way voyaging on the Rarotonga-Atiu-Mitiaro-Mauke axis was across the south-east trade wind in both directions. The pig was in both Rarotonga and Atiu.

On the other hand William Wyatt Gill recorded that the people of Mangaia, a hundred odd miles to windward of the other islands of the Southern Cooks in relation to the prevailing trade wind, had no quadruped other than the rat. He also said that Maretu, the Rarotongan missionary, learnt the Mangaian dialect and traditions in order to be able to perform his ministry among them more adequately.[24] This evidence pointing to the isolation of Mangaia agrees with the fact that it is not in a favourable position for two-way contact with the other islands across the prevailing wind, as Rarotonga, Atiu, Mitiaro, and Mauke are, and that it offers a small target for navigation.

At Aitutaki, which is situated about 146 miles north of Rarotonga, and a lesser distance to the north-west of Atiu, Bligh of
the *Bounty*, the discoverer of Aitutaki, found that the people
knew the name of the pig but had no pigs themselves.[25] John
Williams later corroborated this.[26] Yet the pig was on Atiu as
well as Rarotonga. It would seem that two-way contact between
Aitutaki and Atiu was occasional at most. Again this accords
with their locations in relation to the direction of the prevailing
wind.

Tumu-te-varovaro, the old name for Rarotonga, and Ahuahu,
one name for Mangaia, were in the list of islands known to the
Tahitians given by Tupaea in 1769. Andia, the Spanish captain
who visited Tahiti a few years later, recorded a name which is
plainly that of Atiu.[27] The names of the various islands of the
Southern Cooks could have been brought to Tahiti by one lot
of one-way voyagers, as Cook's associate Anderson suggested,[28]
since Rarotonga, Atiu, Mauke and Mitiaro were in two-way contact, and the names for Mangaia and Aitutaki could no doubt
have been brought to Rarotonga and Atiu by migrants. Alter-
natively the names of the Southern Cooks could have been
brought to Tahiti by several separate lots of one-way voyagers.

Niue is an uplifted atoll about 320 miles west of the Southern
Cooks and 280 miles east of Tonga. The main linguistic and
cultural affinities of its people are Western Polynesian.[29] No
doubt random voyagers from Eastern Polynesia happened
occasionally on the island after it had been settled from Western
Polynesia. The island's name does not appear in the list of
islands known to the Tongans which was collected at the time
of Cook's visit to Tonga in 1777.[30] It is not impossible, however,
that Tongans occasionally showed up at Niue with westerlies
and got back again to their islands with the prevailing wind
from the east.

The last outposts between the central Polynesian islands and
New Zealand and Australia are the Kermadecs and Norfolk

Island, which are situated many hundreds of miles from the nearest inhabited land. They are high, fertile islands, but were uninhabited at the time of their discovery by Europeans. An adze or two, and traces of fireplaces, have been found[31]—mute remains, perhaps, of some involuntary celibates who, like others who left traces on some of the atolls, went off in the fond hope of seeing again the faces of their friends.

In the isolated islands to the south of the central belt, then, as in the atolls to the north, we again see that capricious distribution of population which is so understandable with random settlement and so mysterious from the point of view of deliberate navigation at will. Easter Island, the most isolated, yet a biggish, fertile island, got men and women who decided to stay. Pitcairn, the least isolated, was settled for a time by people who left stone structures and graves. Rapa, a small but fertile island in the oceanic wastes, held migrants who left descendants, and at least one later party which, despite every inducement, decided to go off again. The Kermadecs and Norfolk, though large and fertile, received only early tourists who did not leave their bones for later visitors to find.

Finally there are those islands with Polynesian languages and cultures far to the west of Polynesia, in the eastern sector of the Melanesian islands: Tikopia, Anuta, Rennell, Bellona, Stewart, Ontong Java, the Duffs, and numbers of others.[32] They are scattered among the islands occupied by Melanesians. Rennell and Bellona are even tucked away on the other side of the New Hebrides-Santa Cruz area. The thought that Polynesians, having discovered these islands, went back to Polynesia and took colonizing expeditions to them is unrealistic. The realistic view is that one-way voyagers from Polynesia settled the islands when they were uninhabited.

The first accidental voyages recorded in the Pacific were of Polynesian canoes which Quiros was told had come to the Duffs.[33] Over a period of two to three millennia, it is clear that

The dress of the Maoris, showing their powers of adaptation and invention, exemplifies the evolution of the historical Maori cultures from the culture of the moa-hunter or archaic period. The smoking of cigarettes, like the dressing up of Maori voyaging traditions as history, was a European innovation.

thousands of voyagers must have been borne to Melanesia from
Polynesia with the prevailing winds and currents. The only
ones to leave descendants who were detectably Polynesian, however, would be those who came on uninhabited coasts. It is also
likely that large numbers of Fijians were borne to the Melanesian
islands to the west, but it would be difficult to determine where
this happened.

Raymond Firth, who in 1929 and 1952 made a study of Tiko-
pian voyaging to the satellite island Anuta, sixty miles away,
found that the voyagers set their course by landmarks, waited
for a favourable wind, sailed by night using horizon stars as
guides, and were puzzled when the skies were overcast.[34] Here
is an epitome of the ancient art of Polynesian navigation without instruments, corresponding with the observations of Cook,
Beechey, and others in Polynesia itself (see Chapter Two).

After Tikopia had been settled from Polynesia, contacts developed between it and the Melanesian islands to the west. R. H.
Codrington, an early missionary, recorded that eleven canoes
from Tikopia visited the Banks Islands near the New Hebrides
while he was living there.[35] Tikopia and Vanikoro were in contact in the early nineteenth century, over a gap of more than
100 miles.[36]

Kapingamarangi and Nukuoro, south of the Western Carolines, also had Polynesian languages,[37] as well as Polynesian
canoe designs.[38] Nukuoro was in contact with the Western
Caroline Islands to the north in Kotzebue's time.[39] This shows
that after Nukuoro had been settled by Polynesians, contact
with their Micronesian neighbours developed.

CHAPTER EIGHT

EARLY MAN IN NEW ZEALAND

THE islands of New Zealand have a larger land area than any other Pacific group, and are separated from the rest of Polynesia by distances of many hundreds of miles. A number of interesting questions concerning the early settlement of New Zealand have been obscured by the assumption that the New Zealand Maori ancestors settled the country as deliberate colonists following on its discovery by Polynesian explorers. These questions are discussed in the present chapter.

Anthropologists agree that the basic language and culture of the New Zealand Maoris was derived from Eastern Polynesia, meaning the Polynesian area east of Samoa.[1] It is plain, therefore, that at least one party of migrants including women arrived in New Zealand from Eastern Polynesia in prehistoric times and left descendants. The first permanent settlers, however, may not have been the first human beings in New Zealand. We have seen in Chapter Seven that in historical times there were many uninhabited islands in Polynesia with signs of previous occupation in the form of adzes, charcoal from old fires, graves, ruins of habitations, and even breadfruit trees. If similar episodes of transient occupation by men only, or by men and women who for some reason did not leave descendants, took place in New Zealand before permanent settlement began, there would be no local traditions of their occupation, since there would be no continuing descendants in the country to keep traditions alive. Nor is it likely that signs of these temporary occupants would be left on the surface in later times, because the later, continuing settlers might well have obscured them.

If transient occupants did come to New Zealand in early

times, they need not all have come from Eastern Polynesia. An occasional canoe from Tonga or Fiji could have found its way to New Zealand, since Tonga and Fiji are a great deal nearer to it than are the islands of Eastern Polynesia.

Two possible effects of transient occupation before continuing settlement began are worth keeping in mind. First, aberrant early datings derived from sites of temporary occupation may be made in the future. For evidence of this possibility one need go no farther afield than Norfolk and Pitcairn. They are both reasonably fertile islands with signs of early human occupation, and yet were uninhabited at the time of European contact. If, then, aberrant early datings are made in New Zealand—as elsewhere in the Pacific Islands—they may denote incidents of transient occupation, not necessarily by Eastern Polynesians.

A second possible effect of transient occupation is suggested by the fact that a number of islands in the Pacific had rats but no human inhabitants at the time of European discovery. It is possible, therefore, that the rat was brought to New Zealand by migrants who died out before permanent settlement began. This would not preclude the possibility that rats were introduced by the early permanent settlers also.

The late S. Watson, an authority on the Polynesian rat, told the present author that he did not think rats could have done much to lessen the numbers of the wingless birds of New Zealand, because Polynesian rats on the off-shore islands of New Zealand had not seriously affected the bird populations by destroying eggs. The dog, on the other hand, may have assisted man in the extinction of the moa by running down moa chicks on the plains. Today dogs are powerful destroyers of kiwis if they find them in the forests.

Some evidence from historical times throws light on the circumstances attending the arrival of one-way voyagers in New Zealand in its settlement period. First, a modern map of the Pacific Ocean, published by the National Geographic Society,

Washington, gives a summary in graphic form of the oceanography and meteorology of the South Pacific.[2] This shows a zone
of variable currents and winds between the central belt of Polynesian islands and New Zealand; it is evident therefrom that
canoes could have reached New Zealand by varying courses.
Secondly, two separate derelict canoes of Pacific Islands types
have reached the east coast of New Zealand in the past decade,
one near Auckland, in the Hauraki Gulf area, and one as far
south as Sumner in the South Island.[3] Thirdly, on the Ninety
Mile Beach, on the west coast of the northern peninsula of the
North Island, flotsam from the Pacific Islands, even including
tropical coconut trees with nuts still on them, and woven pan-
danus mats, has been cast up.[4] Canoes could thus have arrived
on the west or east coasts of both islands in prehistoric times.

No one-way voyages in native craft from other islands to New
Zealand appear to have been recorded in historical times, though
many have been in the central belt of Polynesian islands. This
no doubt reflects the fact that New Zealand lies far to the south
of the other islands of Polynesia which were inhabited, and is
separated from them by an area of variable currents and winds.
These facts in their turn indicate that the arrival of men and
women in New Zealand in prehistoric times must have been a
rare event.

Further evidence of the rarity of arrivals of parties including
women is given by the fact that the basic language and culture
of the New Zealand Maoris were Eastern Polynesian. The
traditional place-names reviewed in Chapter Five indicate that
Western Polynesia and Fiji were settled before Eastern Polynesia, and Western Polynesia and Fiji are much nearer to New
Zealand than Eastern Polynesia is. Yet apparently no Western
Polynesian or Fijian settlers including women arrived and established a Western Polynesian or Fijian speech or culture before
permanent settlers from Eastern Polynesia did so.

It was mentioned in Chapter Four that the long one-way
voyages recorded in Polynesia in historical times were invariably

made in isolated canoes, and that this fact is in accord with the obvious difficulties which would have attended attempts by more than one canoe-load of migrants to keep together night after night on such voyages. These difficulties would have been particularly acute on voyages over the great distances and through the variable currents and winds which separate the other Polynesian islands from New Zealand. It is in any case certain that no great numbers of people in prehistoric times ever arrived in New Zealand at the same time.

What light does archaeology throw on the early settlement of New Zealand? Moa-hunter sites with accumulations of graves, archaic adzes, shark-tooth and whale-tooth ornaments, and dog and rat bones have been found in a dozen or more places in the South Island. In some of these sites, North Island obsidian, used for sharp cutting flakes, has been found in quantity, showing that there was communication between the islands. In the North Island also, archaic relics, sometimes in association with moas killed for human food, have been found. Radiocarbon datings which appear to indicate that continuing settlement had commenced by the early centuries of the second millennium A.D., and probably earlier, have been made.[5]

These facts show that an appreciable population had been built up and had spread through both islands within the moa-hunter or archaic period.

It is possible that it was many centuries after the first party of permanent settlers established itself before another party with women came, and that the moa-hunters were derived from this one party. It is in any case unlikely that more than two or three separate parties including women arrived early enough to contribute materially to the formation of the moa-hunter culture. It remains to be seen if archaeology or linguistics can determine whether there were separate arrivals during the settlement period. The archaeology of New Zealand does show, however, that within the moa-hunter or archaic period, the descendants of the formative settlers had spread through the country. Later arrivals could not have initiated any major changes in the language or culture, although they may have introduced one or more useful plants and an adze or two of exotic type. It is not surprising, therefore, that no elements in the later Maori culture which could not have been developed from the archaic culture have been found. The later Maoris were the descendants of the moa-hunters, who were predominantly or exclusively derived from Eastern Polynesia. Maori culture at the time of European contact had evolved from the moa-hunter culture. This follows from the fact that the character of prehistoric Polynesian voyaging did not allow of massive migration over long distances.

In this section the relationship of the New Zealand tribal histories to the facts outlined in the previous sections of the present chapter will be discussed.

In these histories the ancestors of the chiefly families of historical times were described as having come from Hawaiki to the northern parts of the North Island, whence they set off to the various areas of New Zealand which in historical times formed the tribal territories.[6]

The derivation from Hawaiki, as we have seen in Chapter Five, was an adaptation to New Zealand of the general Eastern Polynesian tradition of Savaii in Samoa as the homeland. The stories of the dispersal of the tribes within New Zealand may well derive from traditional memories of the expansion of the early settlers through the country. The story of the Aotea canoe, which is the tribal canoe of the Wanganui-South Taranaki area of the west coast of the North Island, appears to stand somewhat apart from the other tribal canoe traditions and have an archaic flavour, according with the thought that the people of this peripheral area handed on to their descendants a distinctive early canoe tradition. The territories of the Takitimu (or Takitumu) tribal division were distributed along the east coasts of both the North and South Islands. The Tainui and Arawa canoes, from whom most of the New Zealand Maoris claim descent, were traditionally associated with Hauraki Gulf, Tainui going on to Kawhia and Arawa down the east coast. The early missionary J. W. Stack recorded a tradition of a Waitaha tribe in the South Island and said it was associated with the Arawa canoe.[7] The Tokomaru canoe was reputed to have been taken across Auckland isthmus. These traditions may well betoken the dispersal of early settlers from the Hauraki area. This suggestion has some archaeological evidence in its favour, since numbers of archaic adzes have been found in the Hauraki area.

Hare Hongi (Henry Stowell), who was taught by priests of the Ngapuhi tribe in the north of New Zealand in the seventies of last century, partially anticipated the interpretations of the New Zealand tribal traditions given in the previous paragraph when he said that there was no migration to New Zealand in a fleet and that the tribal leaders who were reputed to have arrived in the fleet were New Zealand-born ancestors round whom fables had been woven.[8] Some of them, however, appear to have been heroes of Western Polynesian folk-lore (see Chapter Five). Perhaps some were Tongan or Samoan ancestors.

A vital chapter in Maori history, the early moa-hunter or archaic phase described in the previous section, has become obscure in Maori tradition. Reasons for this are given in the following paragraph.

In 1843-1844 Edward Shortland, a Government emissary, was told by the chiefs in the south of the South Island of how the Ngati-Mamoe tribe had been defeated several centuries earlier by invaders from the north, a new tribe being formed eventually by the merging of the older remnants with the conquerors. 'I found,' wrote Shortland, 'that all the families of the present day, of any consideration, traced their origin to the Turanga, or Poverty Bay sources—as being the conquering side, and therefore the more honourable—and neglected altogether the Ngati-mamoe sources, beyond the time of their conquest.'[9] Such practices, repeated over several centuries, would mean that the early history of the Maoris before the tribal divisions developed would tend to be shortened and forgotten. Nowhere in the whole body of Maori tribal history is there any genealogy of a defeated previous family. All the surviving genealogies are of the families which were still in power in historical times.

The Maori tribal divisions were of course real in later times. But the community of blood and culture in the Maoris was and is much more pronounced than their divisions.

The Chatham Islands lie some 600 miles east of the main islands of New Zealand, in a zone where westerlies are frequent. Unnavigated voyages from the main islands of New Zealand account for the early settlement of the Chathams. H. D. Skinner and others have demonstrated that the older culture of the Chathams is basically related to the moa-hunter culture of New Zealand.[10] Evidence of the way in which the Chathams were settled is given by the fact that when John Williams, having taken a passage in a sailing ship, was in sight of the New Zealand coast, the ship was blown 300 miles to the east, which is halfway to the Chathams.[11] There is no evidence that any voyager ever got back from the Chathams to New Zealand in pre-European times, much less sailed back to the Chathams. There were no dogs in the Chathams at the time of European contact.[12] After the Chathams were permanently settled by one-way voyagers from the main islands of New Zealand in moa-hunter times, later casual migrants no doubt arrived from those islands. The adzes of late North Island type which have been found in the Chathams can thus be explained by later diffusion.[13] It is also not impossible that random migrants from other Polynesian islands turned up in the Chathams after they had been settled in New Zealand moa-hunter times.

It would seem that when the early settlers of New Zealand reached its distant shores, they approached as near as human beings ever have to the ideal state in which some romantic writers imagine early man to have lived. They hunted moas, pigeons, and other succulent birds, caught groper, cod, shark, seal, and porpoise, had a very good stone for their adzes, and were free of natural enemies. They had plenty of room to expand, and little competition as yet from their own kind. The scenery was magnificent, with many high, snow-clad mountains and swift rivers. Innumerable birds saluted the rising sun, as they were doing when Cook's associate Banks noted the fact centuries later.[14] The people told their children of the traditional homeland in far Savaii, where Tupa and his relatives had done wondrous things. An occasional shaking of the earth reminded them of the wrath of the gods, and sacred mountains flashing fire were their visible embodiment. The New Zealand Maoris were the descendants of a long succession of one-way voyagers from Asia itself, and were healthy, hardy, and optimistic, taking life as it came, as their forebears who were borne to distant islands had done many times before them.

CHAPTER NINE

THE POLYNESIAN MIGRATION TRAIL

No question has caused more wonderment, or more debate, than the question of the Polynesian migration trail. Nobody any longer seriously contends that the Polynesians came through continents or chains of islands that have since disappeared,[1] because the geologists have shown that, apart from New Zealand, which has itself been separated from other land for many thousands of years, the Polynesian islands, like most of the other Pacific islands, were formed by volcanoes which rose from the sea floor.[2] Several writers in the nineteenth and twentieth centuries have thought that the Polynesians, or most of them, arrived in their islands from the Americas.[3] This view has found scant support from most Pacific scholars.[4] These scholars, however, have held divergent views on whether the Polynesians came from the west by way of Melanesia or Micronesia.[5] The lush Tahitian islands have been thought of as the main early colony within Eastern Polynesia which the Eastern Polynesian ancestors would have sought out and settled, and from which the other Eastern Polynesian groups, as well as Hawaii and New Zealand, were colonized.[6]

The opinion that the Pacific Islands were settled from America was put forward by J. de Zuñiga, a Spanish missionary in the Philippines, in a book first published in 1803. His main reason for holding this opinion was that the prevailing winds and currents come from the east. William Ellis, for the same reason, argued a generation later that the eastern groups of Polynesia had been peopled from America. In recent years Thor Heyerdahl has also put forward the view that the Polynesians came into their islands from the Americas. He places emphasis on the prevailing winds and currents from the east, but also uses evidence from blood groups, botanical and cultural affinities, the capacities of Inca rafts, and Peruvian legends of the disappearance of the chief Kon-Tiki (Con-Ticci) into the Pacific. He has stated for example that the Lake Titicaca and Easter Island reed are of the same species, and that the reed was imported into Easter Island from Peru as a material for reed boats; that the sweet potato came into the Pacific from Chile or Peru with Easter Island as the main gateway; and that other Andean plants, including Chile peppers, were on Easter Island in prehistoric times. He has also argued that, because he and some associates, in excavations on the Galapagos Islands, found pottery corresponding to several ancient pottery epochs on the Peru-Ecuador coast several hundred miles away, voyagers on the latter coast had paid repeated visits to the Galapagos Islands in prehistoric times, the implication being that they possessed the vessels and maritime arts to get to Easter Island.[7] He has, however, emphasized that he accepts the theory that there was an Indonesian origin behind the present Polynesian race and culture, but has said that he believes that the Indonesian migrants came, not through Melanesia or Micronesia, but by the route farther north with the Japan Current to America, and thence to Polynesia.[8]

Zuñiga, Ellis, and Heyerdahl, in emphasizing that the prevailing winds and currents come from the east in the Pacific islands, overlook the fact that westerlies blow fitfully in the summer months all the way from the East Indies to Polynesia. The double canoes and outrigger canoes which were the standard Polynesian vessels in early historical times were fully capable of bringing the Polynesian ancestors from the west through Melanesia or Micronesia by a succession of one-way migrations during westerlies (see Chapter Three). The pigs of Polynesia did not come from America, but are of Asiatic and East Indies origin. They could not have swum across the larger gaps, yet they got as far as the Marquesas Group and Hawaii. Clearly the prevailing winds and currents from the east were not an obstacle to the dispersal throughout the high groups of the Pacific of the pig, or of the men and women whom it must have accompanied.

As evidence of the American derivation of the Polynesians, Heyerdahl has made much of a statement by R. T. Simmons and J. J. Graydon of the Australian Commonwealth Serum Laboratory that 'there is a close blood genetic relationship between American Indians and Polynesians, and that no similar relationship is evident when Polynesians are compared with Melanesians, Micronesians, and Indonesians, except mainly in adjacent areas of contact'.[9] This statement, however, contrasts with Simmons's and Graydon's own evidence that the Diego blood factor is possessed by American Indians but not Polynesians, and begs the question of whether blood factor B was absent from the Eastern Polynesians, although present in Western Polynesians, because the Eastern Polynesians were descended from a small party of Western Polynesians who happened not to transmit the gene for type B to their progeny. In a later paper, given at the Tenth Pacific Science Congress in 1961, Simmons conceded that 'blood group serology does not prove to us who they [the Polynesians] were or from whence they came', and added that 'it seems evident that there were no planned migrations into Polynesia, and that the Polynesian people spread mainly by accidental voyages to all the distant Polynesian islands'. He still maintained, however, that the Polynesian ancestors lacked blood group B and that the Western Polynesians acquired it by later gene flow from Melanesia and Micronesia.[10] E. Goldschmidt, an American anthropologist, at the same congress, stated that if, in accordance with a recent theory, the settlement of Polynesia is viewed as the result of a succession of small colonizing units, then the random selection of people with varying gene frequencies is likely to have occurred.[11]

According to the geneticist W. C. Boyd, external bodily features such as skin pigmentation, hair colour and form, and skull shape are too variable among Pacific peoples to be reliable indicators of origins.[12] Heyerdahl's use of the legends of the white-skinned, red-haired followers of Kon-Tiki and the sporadic occurrence of light skin and red hair in some Polynesians, therefore, are not significant.

The American and Polynesian peoples, languages and cultures were neither more nor less like one another than others known to have been derived either from a third area or independently. The compilation of a number of resemblances between arts and crafts, stone monuments, and customs cannot of itself establish whether one of two cultures came from the other directly, or both from a third area, or whether some of their common features were developed independently because of similar environments. The cultural resemblances used by Heyerdahl as evidence that the Polynesians came from the Americas are thus inconclusive.

Heyerdahl's contention that the reed was imported from Peru into Easter Island as a material for reed boats is another overstatement. Sedges are remarkably capricious in their distribution. There is, for instance, a Northern Hemisphere species which, in the Southern Hemisphere, grows only in New Zealand.[13] Reed boats were also used by the New Zealand Maoris.[14] These facts, however, do not mean that this reed was imported into New Zealand by man in a past age.

When Heyerdahl's overstatements have been discounted, some respectable evidence remains for the view that casual migrants occasionally arrived in Polynesia from America.

First, although the previously accepted view that the sweet potato was of American origin was called in question by the botanist E. D. Merrill,[15] recent research by the botanist D. E. Yen indicates that the sweet potato came into Polynesia from America, probably with men, although Yen makes the reservation that it might have been brought by seed-carrying birds.[16]

Cumar, the Quichua Indian word for sweet potato, closely resembles the Polynesian name, and was recorded in Ecuador by the botanist Seemann in the first half of the nineteenth century;[17] it is difficult to believe that the word was introduced into Ecuador from Polynesia in post-European times. The present author used to think it possible that Polynesian voyagers, having reached America, might have pushed off again with American plants and got back to somewhere or other in Polynesia.[18] Yen has also suggested that Polynesians may have selected the sweet potato in America because of its resemblance to their other vegetatively propagated plants. Since, however, Eric de Bisschop failed on both legs of his attempt to get to America from Polynesia and back again (see Chapter Three), despite the advantage of modern geographical knowledge and navigation aids in keeping to a direct plotted course, this idea loses its attraction. (If there is other evidence of human contact with the Americas from Polynesia, it is compatible with one-way voyages from Polynesia to the east with the westerlies of higher latitudes.) The evidence of the sweet potato and its name, therefore, creates the presumption that migrants from America brought the plant to Eastern Polynesia after the Polynesians were established in the eastern islands. It does not follow, however, that the plant arrived first in Easter Island, rather than in the Marquesas Group or elsewhere in Eastern Polynesia. If Chile peppers were introduced into Easter Island from America by men in prehistoric times, as Heyerdahl suggests, then this would also be compatible with occasional migration from the Americas to Polynesia.

Secondly, types of cotton which botanical analysis shows to be the result of crossing between Old World and American strains were found growing wild by early European visitors to the Tahitian and Hawaiian Islands.[19] Perhaps the seeds were conveyed by casual migrants from America, who arrived before the Polynesians but did not leave descendants. This could explain why the plants were growing wild.

Thirdly, Heyerdahl's argument that, because he and his companions found pottery in the Galapagos Islands corresponding to several distinct pottery epochs on the Peru-Ecuador coast, voyagers from Peru and Ecuador had sailed deliberately to and from the Galapagos Islands, is an overstatement, because the archaeological evidence in the Galapagos Islands can be explained by several separate and disconnected arrivals of one-way migrants who did not leave descendants. But this explanation strengthens rather than weakens Heyerdahl's case for one-way migration from South America to Polynesia.

Fourthly, indirect evidence that craft might have made one-way voyages from America to Polynesia is given by the pine logs which the Hawaiians found on their shores and used for canoes, by a derelict ship which drifted from off the South American coast to Eastern Polynesia, and by Heyerdahl's own one-way voyage on the Kon-Tiki raft.[20]

On the other hand, there are good reasons for believing that the arrivals of American Indian migrants in Polynesia would be few and far between. There are few islands near the American coast to encourage the development of off-shore voyaging. South American coastal journeys were made in a particularly settled weather area. Continental coasts are different from those of islands, because the voyager knows whether he is east or west of home, and in making back can depend on reaching the coast somewhere if he survives. At night sea breezes blow shoreward. Off the American coast the prevailing winds and currents toward the west do not become strong until one is well out to sea. It is probable, therefore, that only exiles who were particularly determined to get to the west would reach Polynesia. There is no necessity, therefore, to think that women came from America to Polynesia over distances of thousands of miles before women arrived from the west by a series of far shorter migrations.

The basic affinities of the Polynesian, Melanesian, Micronesian and Indonesian speeches,[21] the similarity of the Melanesian, Micronesian and Polynesian craft, the great preponderance of

Polynesian cultivated plants which were not indigenous to America, and the presence of the pig from the East Indies to the Marquesas Group and Hawaii, are best explained by the view that the decisive primary settlers of Polynesia came from the west and not via the Americas. But there is also good reason to believe that occasional one-way migrants came from the Americas.

Some early European observers who thought that the Polynesian ancestors migrated from the west put forward in crude form the theory that they came through Melanesia.[22] An American linguist, G. W. Grace, recently argued that the Fijian, Polynesian and Rotuman languages derive from a common ancestral language which had itself come from Melanesian islands west of Fiji. He cited innovations shared by the Fijian, Polynesian and Rotuman languages but not, in his opinion, by other languages.[23] But I. Dyen, another expert in the speeches of Oceania, has called in question the exclusive character of Grace's shared innovations. Dyen, having found that the basic words of the Melanesian languages show that these languages have developed considerable diversity among themselves, has suggested that the Malayo-Polynesian language family, to which the Polynesian, Micronesian and most of the East Indies-Formosa speeches also belong, evolved in Melanesia, although he concedes that some of the speeches of Formosa, and one speech in the Sumatra area, show considerable divergence from the other Malayo-Polynesian speeches of the East Indies-Formosa archipelago.[24]

Robert C. Suggs, citing Grace's view that the Polynesian speeches were of Melanesian origin, has supported it with archaeological evidence in Melanesia and Polynesia, but Suggs's use of this evidence has been challenged by J. Golson, a British archaeologist.[25] Suggs, moreover, overlooked the fact that part of Grace's hypothesis was that the Micronesian languages nearest to Polynesia also derived from Melanesia. If that were so,

DRINKING CEREMONY IN EASTERN FIJI

Public Relations Office, Fiji

The Polynesians could have come from Polynesian-like people in
Melanesia.

then such cultural affinities as archaeology could show to exist between Melanesia and Polynesia might in theory have been mediated through the Micronesian areas nearest Polynesia.

A number of theorists, assuming that peoples differing in stock and culture from the Polynesians had filled Melanesia, have thought that the Polynesian ancestors later by-passed that area. Peter Buck and other anthropologists have favoured the Micronesian chain of islands leading from the East Indies through the Caroline and Gilbert Islands to the threshold of Polynesia as the Polynesian migration route.[26] Buck argued that this view was supported by the fact that the Micronesians and Polynesians had some cultural features in common.

The idea that the inhabitants of New Guinea, the Solomons and Fiji were markedly different from the Polynesians in earlier times is not sustained by the evidence of early observers. William Wyatt Gill, who visited New Guinea in 1872, when it was still little known, found the south-eastern parts solidly occupied by people who he said were very similar to the Samoans and Rarotongans, and who had a number of basic words with Rarotongan equivalents. On the other hand, to the west of the Polynesian-like people, toward the Torres Strait area, there were people with black skins and fuzzy hair. So marked was the difference between these two groups of neighbouring people that a black man who had come among the Polynesian-like people looked strange. Gill's view was that the Polynesians derived from the Polynesian-like people in the New Guinea area. He considered that the language of the Gilbertese whom he met on a visit to the Gilberts was markedly different from that of the Polynesians.[27]

The fact that the differences between the peoples of eastern New Guinea in the twentieth century were no longer so pronounced as Gill found them to be in the nineteenth shows the danger of thinking that the present state of affairs in the East Indies, New Guinea and Melanesia was the same several thousand years ago as it is today.

I

Divergences in physical type were found among the peoples south-east of New Guinea also. When the Spaniards of Mendaña's second expedition across the Pacific discovered Ndeni (Santa Cruz), lying between the Solomons and New Hebrides, in 1595, they saw there tawny people as well as black. Quiros, the chief pilot, was told by some of the members of the expedition who had accompanied Mendaña on his first voyage that the people in the Solomons whom they had seen then were like those of Ndeni.[28]

Fiji is another area where the people's appearance was not uniform in former times. When William Bligh in 1789 passed Ngau, in the western sector of Fiji, he said that the men who came out to the ship in two canoes were 'rather lighter-coloured' than the Tahitians.[29] Those who assume that the Polynesians and Fijians arrived in their islands by different routes and that the light-skinned strains among the Fijians were the result of later Polynesian infiltrations are influenced by the allied assumption that the Polynesian ancestors came in substantial numbers by planned migrations.

When the idea of fairly massive waves of migration from the west into Melanesia, Micronesia and Polynesia is replaced by the more realistic view that a few people at a time were conveyed from group to group by westerlies over a long period, both the divergences and similarities between the peoples of the Pacific Islands are simply explained by the view that random selections took place. It is evident, therefore, that the Polynesians could have come from anywhere in Melanesia, or in Micronesia, so far as the physical appearance of the inhabitants of Melanesia, Micronesia, and Polynesia at the time of early European contact with the inhabitants of those areas is concerned.

Buck, in support of his view that the Polynesian ancestors came through the Micronesian chain, cited cultural evidence. Thus he stated that the Gilbertese wore helmets of Cook Islands type.[30] But these features might have been brought by accidental voyagers from Polynesia, like those who came in Gill's time from the Cook Islands to the Ellice Islands (see Chapter Four). (R. P. Lesson, the naturalist on Duperrey's voyage in 1822-1825, thought that the people of the Micronesian area were partly Mongols, and noted that some of the inhabitants of the Gilberts and southern Marshall Islands wore headgear of Chinese type.)[31] Buck also said that the people of Micronesia used slings in their wars, whereas the Melanesians used bows and arrows.[32] But Cook was told that the Fijians, some of whom he met in Tonga, used slings as well as bows and arrows,[33] and George Brown, an early missionary in the islands near New Guinea, said that in large areas the bow was unknown.[34] Some of these cultural similarities may be explained by later diffusion from island to island after the times of original settlement. If so, then cultural characteristics of this kind are unreliable as tests of sources of original settlement. Analogies with most Polynesian cultural features, and with most Micronesian ones, can be found some-where or other in Melanesia. So far as cultural evidence goes, it is no less possible that the Micronesians, as well as the Poly-nesians, came for the most part from Melanesia than that the Polynesians came from Micronesia.

The view of the present author is that the Polynesian ancestors came from the west through the waters between Buru and Yap to eastern New Guinea and the Melanesian islands and thence to Polynesia by a slow succession of west-east voyages. (B. Hilder, an Australian sea-captain with long experience in the Pacific, has cited a random one-way voyage in 1947 of some islanders from the Sangir-Moluccas area of the East Indies to the Vitu Islands east of New Guinea, a distance of 1,500 miles to the south-east.)[35] It is probable that, as the result of the combined effects of later warfare and secondary east-west settlement, linguistic and ethnological indications of the thin threads of primary west-east migration from Asia have become obscure. The fact that the Fijians and Western Polynesians maintained a specially close relationship with their maternal uncles and aunts and used the same basic word to describe this relationship is easier to explain by the view that the Fijian and Polynesian ancestors shared a common kinship system somewhere in Melanesia than by Buck's suggestion that the Polynesians borrowed this feature from Fiji after their arrival from Micronesia.

We come now to the question of the Polynesian migration trail within Polynesia itself. The conventional view that Samoa and Tahiti were the primary Western Polynesian and Eastern Polynesian centres of settlement and further dispersal is based on the assumption that Polynesian explorers sought out these fertile, centrally situated islands. The preferred hypothesis of the present author is that the Samoans were predominantly or exclusively derived from Tonga and the Marquesans from eastern Savaii, and that the Eastern Polynesians, Hawaiians, and New Zealand Maoris descended from the early Marquesans. Reasons for this hypothesis are given in the remainder of this chapter.

In Chapter Five traditional place-names pointing to the Samoan island of Savaii as the traditional homeland of the Eastern Polynesians, Hawaiians, and New Zealand Maoris were reviewed. The tradition of Hawaiki and dialectal equivalents of this name was one of the features which distinguished the eastern cultures of Polynesia from the western.[36]

S. H. Elbert, an American linguist, in a study published in 1953, concluded that the ancestors of the Eastern Polynesians, Hawaiians, and New Zealand Maoris must have lived together for some centuries outside Western Polynesia. Thus forty-six words found in at least two Eastern Polynesian languages were not found at all in the western islands with Polynesian speeches.[37]

In 1956 to 1958 Robert C. Suggs carried out an impressive series of archaeological excavations in the Marquesas Group, on the north-eastern fringe of Eastern Polynesia.[38] This group lies 2,000 miles to the east of Samoa, with only a few low, small atolls in between. At Ha'atuatua Bay, on the east coast of the Marquesan island of Nuku Hiva, Suggs secured a radiocarbon dating of human occupation in or around the first century B.C. This was the earliest date he obtained among various sites that he investigated in the Marquesas Group. It is also the earliest radiocarbon dating so far obtained anywhere in Eastern Polynesia. J. Golson, during excavations on Upolu, the Samoan island to the east of Savaii, had previously secured a radiocarbon dating of human occupation in association with pottery somewhere round the birth of Christ.[39] Suggs also found a few pieces of pottery at Ha'atuatua. The occupation of the Ha'atuatua site had lasted for several centuries. Its early occupants had stone adzes of various distinctive shapes—those which predominated showed close affinities with Western Polynesian types. There were also pig, dog and rat bones, shell scrapers adapted for scraping coconut, and shell peeling knives of a type used elsewhere for peeling breadfruit and edible roots, presumably indicating that the early settlers of Ha'atuatua had one or more such plants. A number of graves were found round an archaic altar. From his archaeological evidence, Suggs formed the opinion that the early culture of Nuku Hiva was derived from Western Polynesia.

The following reconstruction is offered by the present author. Within the barrier reef off the eastern coast of the main Samoan island of Savaii lie several villages, including Iva. There, many centuries ago, in a part of Savaii particularly suited to human settlement, Samoans had already been living for some time. At that juncture some people from eastern Savaii reached the Marquesas Group. They may have been would-be colonists who, dissatisfied with the increasing competition from their neighbours, set out for the islands in the east of the Samoa Group with livestock, plants and household goods, and after losing their bearings eventually got to the Marquesas Group with the help of recurring westerlies. They may have been voluntary exiles who set off into the Pacific wastes in the hope of finding other land.

They called the Marquesan island on which they settled Iva or Hiva, after their home in eastern Savaii. Their descendants multiplied, and in due course spread throughout Eastern Polynesia by one-way voyages, finding its various groups still uninhabited because of the rarity of west-east voyages. Hawaii and New Zealand were settled from Eastern Polynesia by one-way voyages.

There is historical evidence of the capacity of westerlies to bear Pacific Islanders to the east. Gill told of the 'numerous family' who were conveyed from the Tokelaus to Mangaia via Nassau and Palmerston, a distance of 1,250 miles, and Beechey of the men, women and children who were borne from near the Tahitian islands to an island 600 miles to the east (see Chapter Three). In Dillon's time a one-way voyager from Rotuma was borne to Samoa, 600 miles to the east.[40] When Kotzebue visited the Marshall Group in 1817, he met there two Caroline Islanders who some years before had been blown west of their home island, had tried for five months to get back, and had eventually finished up on an island 2,000 miles east of their home island, still thinking themselves west of it.[41] This incident points up the inability of voyagers to keep track of longitude in the days before instruments. Kotzebue's Caroline Islanders were probably helped on their way by the north equatorial counter-current which sets to the east. A similar aid to the Western Polynesian settlers of the Marquesas Group may have been the east-setting counter-current which a map of the Pacific recently issued by the National Geographic Society shows in the latitude of the northern part of the Marquesas Group.[42]

We have seen earlier in the present chapter that a negligible number of Eastern Polynesians, Hawaiians, and New Zealand Maoris of full blood are of blood group B, whereas substantial numbers of Western Polynesians, Melanesians, and Micronesians are of this blood group. If the Eastern Polynesians, Hawaiians, and New Zealand Maoris were derived from a small number of people of the same family group who came from Savaii and failed, as the result of their random selection, to retain and transmit the gene for blood type B to their descendants, the absence of blood group B among these peoples is explained.

Elbert's finding that the Samoan speech is simpler than Tongan and that the Eastern Polynesian speeches are simpler than Samoan[43] is in conformity with the view that Samoa was initially settled by a small number of Tongans, and Eastern Polynesia by a small number of Samoans.

Most of the traditional place-names mentioned in Chapter Five have their equivalents in Marquesan tradition. It is noteworthy that the Marquesan traditional place-name Temoe is identical with the name of Mangareva's satellite island, and that the name of an island close to Nuku Hiva in the Marquesas Group, Ua Pou, appears to be an ancient Mangarevan place-name.[44] These facts accord with the view that the early Marquesan settlers came from Samoa and that their descendants in due course settled the other Eastern Polynesian groups, Hawaii, and New Zealand, taking their traditional place-names with them.

The preferred view of the present author is that the Marquesans descended from a few survivors of a one-way voyage from eastern Savaii to Nuku Hiva about 2,000 years ago, and that the effective settlers of Hawaii, Easter Island, the Tahitian islands and Mangareva were Marquesan one-way voyagers who set out in the hope of finding traditional islands. The early settlers of Nuku Hiva made innovations in their artifacts, including the manufacture of one-piece fishhooks. They probably began to tang some of their adzes as an aid to lashing them to the handles —tanged adzes were a minority of the adzes Suggs found at Ha'atuatua—and in due course the tanging of adzes was widely diffused to other islands. Within a few centuries of the settlement of the Marquesas Group casual migrants from America probably brought the sweet potato to that group, whence Marquesan migrants distributed it to other Eastern Polynesian groups, Hawaii, and New Zealand. The art of harpooning was probably diffused in the same way to other groups including New Zealand.[45] The Marquesas Group is the most favourably placed of the Polynesian islands for one-way voyages to Hawaii, and there is some archaeological evidence that the early Hawaiians had shared a common culture with the early Marquesans.[46] It is also probable from the direction of the prevailing winds and currents that after the Tahitian islands had been settled from the Marquesas Group descendants of the early Tahitian settlers settled the Southern Cooks and, either directly or by way of the Southern Cooks or both, New Zealand. The archaeologist Y. H. Sinoto recently found in the western sector of the Tahitian islands a grave of an adult male buried in the same fashion as that practised by the New Zealand moa-hunters, with bonito fishhooks and whale-tooth pendants identical with archaic New Zealand types.[47]

The attraction of Pacific prehistory is that of a series of fascinating 'whodunits', the attempted solution of which gives many people interest and pleasure. Long may the attempts continue!

SOURCES

CHAPTER ONE: A WORLD PERSPECTIVE

1. For Cook's and Anderson's evidence on Cook's third voyage to the Pacific, J. Cook, *A Voyage to the Pacific Ocean* (London, 1784), vol. i, pp. 167-224, 367-379, vol. ii, pp. 1-178.

2. H. Carrington, *Life of Captain Cook* (London, 1939), p. 59; C. de Brosses, *Histoire des navigations aux terres australes* (Paris, 1756), vol. ii, pp. 443-445.

3. For discovery of Atlantic and Indian Ocean islands, *Encyclopaedia Britannica* under names of islands.

4. For relevant extracts from sagas mentioned in this chapter, H. G. Leach, *Pageant of Old Scandinavia* (Princeton, 1946), pp. 129, 277, 282-289.

5. For review of Greenland archaeology, V. Stefansson, *Greenland* (London, 1943), pp. 77-143.

6. M. Flinders, *A Voyage to Terra Australis* (London, 1814), vol. ii, pp. 228-233.

7. *Dominion*, Wellington, 21 March 1960.

8. A. Capell, 'A New Approach to Australian Linguistics', *Oceania Linguistic Monographs 1*.

9. *Australian Encyclopaedia* (Sydney, 1958), vol. i, pp. 9-12.

10. O. von Kotzebue, *Voyage of Discovery in the South Sea* (London, 1821), vol. iii, pp. 122-123, 135.

11. W. H. Goodenough, 'Oceania and the Problem of Controls in the Study of Cultural and Human Evolution', *Journal of the Polynesian Society*, vol. lxvi, pp. 152-153; T. Gladwin, 'Canoe Travel in the Truk Area: Technology and its Psychological Correlates', *American Anthropologist*, vol. lx, pp. 893-899.

12. Summaries are given in *Ergebnisse der Südsee-Expedition 1908-10*, II B, vols. v-xi (Hamburg, 1932-8), navigation sections.

13. Kotzebue, op. cit., vol. ii, pp. 144-146, end-chart, vol. iii, pp. 118-119, 177-180, end-chart; H. Nevermann, *Ergebnisse der Südsee-Expedition 1908-10*, II B, vol. xi (Hamburg, 1938), pp. 217, 221-230.

14. C. Wilkes, *Narrative of the United States Exploring Expedition during the Years 1838, 1839, 1840, 1841 and 1842* (Philadelphia,

1845), vol. v, pp. 37-108; H. Hale, *United States Exploring Expedition. . . . Ethnography and Philology* (Philadelphia, 1846), pp. 69-103, 161-167.

15. H. E. Maude, 'The Colonization of the Phoenix Islands', *Journal of the Polynesian Society*, vol. lxi, p. 81.

16. E. Sabatier, *Sous l'équateur du Pacifique: les îles Gilbert* (Paris, 1939), pp. 26-27.

17. E. G. Burrows, 'Ethnology of Uvea', *Bishop Museum Bulletin 145*, p. 171.

18. J. Martin (ed.), *An Account of the Natives of the Tonga Islands* (London, 1817), vol. i, p. 323; P. Dillon, *Narrative . . . of a Voyage in the South Seas* (London, 1829), vol. i, pp. 294-295, vol. ii, pp. 78-79.

19. G. Turner, *Nineteen Years in Polynesia* (London, 1861), p. 270.

20. Hale, op. cit., p. 165.

21. For information given to Cook and associates on his first voyage by Tupaea and other Tahitians, J. Cook, *The Journals of Captain James Cook*, ed. J. C. Beaglehole, vol. i (Hakluyt Society, 1955), pp. 291-294; J. R. Forster, *Observations made during a Voyage round the World* (London, 1778), pp. 511-525.

22. Cook, op. cit., pp. 155-157.

23. L. A. de Bougainville, *A Voyage round the World* (London, 1772), pp. 268-269.

24. B. G. Corney (ed.), *The Quest and Occupation of Tahiti by Emissaries of Spain* (Hakluyt Society, 1913-18), vol. i, p. 354, vol. ii, pp. 187-189, 284-287.

CHAPTER TWO: HOW DID THE POLYNESIANS NAVIGATE?

1. J. Cook, *A Voyage to the Pacific Ocean* (London, 1784), vol. i, pp. 368-376, vol. ii, pp. 142-143; Corney, op. cit., vol. ii, pp. 187-189, 284-287.

2. J. Williams, *A Narrative of Missionary Enterprises in the South Sea Islands* (London, 1837), pp. 96-97.

3. F. W. Beechey, *Narrative of a Voyage* (London, 1831), vol. i, p. 169.

4. R. C. Suggs, *The Island Civilizations of Polynesia* (New York, 1960), pp. 83-84; R. Duff, 'The Origins of the Maori', *N.Z. Listener*, 9 February 1962, p. 7.

5. E. Best, 'The Astronomical Knowledge of the Maori', *Dominion Museum Monograph 3*, pp. 228-229.

6. E. Best, 'Polynesian Voyagers. The Maori as a Deep-sea Navigator, Explorer, and Colonizer', *Dominion Museum Monograph 5*.

7. For Gatty's views on Polynesian navigation, H. Gatty, *Nature is Your Guide* (London, 1958), pp. 29-54, 81-93, 154-223.

8. E. de Bisschop, *Tahiti-Nui* (London, 1959), pp. 43-45.

9. National Geographic Society, 'Pacific Ocean', Atlas Plate 61 (Washington, 1962).

10. Hydrographic Department, Admiralty, *Pacific Islands Pilot*, vol. ii (1943), pp. 3-7, vol. iii (1946), pp. 16-19.

11. G. H. Heyen, 'Primitive Navigation in the Pacific—I', in 'Polynesian Navigation', *Polynesian Society Memoir 34*, pp. 64-79.

12. J. Bollons, 'Polynesian Navigators: a Seaman's View', *New Zealand Herald*, 24 May 1924, supplement, p. 1; editorial note, 'The Polynesians as Navigators', *Journal of the Polynesian Society*, vol. xxxiii, pp. 221-222.

13. B. Hilder, 'Primitive Navigation in the Pacific—II', in 'Polynesian Navigation', *Polynesian Society Memoir 34*, pp. 81-97.

14. G. S. Parsonson, 'The Settlement of Oceania: an Examination of the Accidental Voyage Theory', in 'Polynesian Navigation', *Polynesian Society Memoir 34*, pp. 11-63; G. M. Dening, 'The Geographical Knowledge of the Polynesians and the Nature of Inter-Island Contact', in 'Polynesian Navigation', *Polynesian Society Memoir 34*, pp. 102-131.

15. H. Rodman, 'The Sacred Calabash', *Journal of the Polynesian Society*, vol. xxxvii, pp. 75-85

16. J. F. G. Stokes, note in *Journal of the Polynesian Society*, vol. xxxvii, pp. 85-87.

17. H. Stowell, Stowell papers no. 30, Alexander Turnbull Library.

18. S. P. Smith, *Hawaiki* (Wellington, 1910), p. 188.

19. J. Williams, op. cit., p. 76.

20. W. W. Gill, 'The Origin of the Island Manihiki', *Journal of the Polynesian Society*, vol. xxiv, pp. 144-145.

21. L. C. de Freycinet, *Voyage autour du monde* (Paris, 1824-44), vol. ii, pp. 81-82.

22. Martin, op. cit., vol. ii, pp. 48-50.

23. Suggs, op. cit., pp. 80-81.

24. E.g., ibid., p. 81.

CHAPTER THREE: STONE AGE VESSELS IN THE PACIFIC

1. For summary of historical evidence, J. Hornell, 'Canoes of Oceania', vol. i, *Bishop Museum Special Publication 27*.
2. W. T. Pritchard, *Polynesian Reminiscences* (London, 1866), pp. 390, 403.
3. Dillon, op. cit., vol. ii, pp. 104-106.
4. Cook, op. cit., vol. ii, pp. 142-143.
5. J. Morrison, *The Journal of James Morrison* (Golden Cockerel Press, 1935), p. 201.
6. Martin, op. cit., pp. 73-76, 317-347.
7. Dillon, op. cit., vol. i, p. 295, vol. ii, pp. 102-103, 111, 133.
8. W. Ellis, *Polynesian Researches* (London, 1831), vol. i, pp. 164-165.
9. C. O. Bechtol, 'Sailing Characteristics of Oceanic Canoes', in 'Polynesian Navigation', *Polynesian Society Memoir 34*, pp. 98-101.
10. Kotzebue, op. cit., vol. ii, pp. 240-241, vol. iii, pp. 111-112; Freycinet, op. cit., vol. ii, pp. 102, 131.
11. E. de Bisschop, *The Voyage of the Kaimiloa* (London, 1940); *Tahiti-Nui* (London, 1958), pp. 30-43.
12. T. Heyerdahl, *The Kon-Tiki Expedition* (London, 1950).
13. De Bisschop, op. cit., pp. 13-14, 48, 52-53.
14. T. Heyerdahl, 'Guara Navigation: Indigenous Sailing off the Andean Coast', *Southwestern Journal of Anthropology*, vol. xii, pp. 134-143.
15. De Bisschop, op. cit.
16. E. Danielsson, *From Raft to Raft* (London, 1960).

CHAPTER FOUR: VOYAGES OF NO RETURN

1. For biographical details of Williams, E. Prout, *Memoirs of the Life of the Rev. John Williams* (London, 1843).
2. J. Williams, op. cit., pp. 76, 143-151.
3. Turner, op. cit., p. 490.
4. J. Williams, op. cit., pp. 76, 143-151, 410-411, 466-468, 504-507.
5. Gill, op. cit., p. 145.
6. Dillon, op. cit., vol. i, pp. 271-273.
7. For Ellis's accounts of voyages referred to, Ellis, op. cit., vol. i, p. 170, vol. iii, pp. 371, 374, 376, 390, 393, 396-397, 400; *Narrative of a Tour through Hawaii* (London, 1827), p. 442.

8. Ellis, op. cit., p. 442; *Polynesian Researches* (London, 1831), pp. 125-127.

9. S. Dibble, *History of the Sandwich Islands* (New York, 1839), pp. 16-17.

10. Turner, op. cit., pp. 359-360.

11. Ibid., pp. 391-392.

12. Beechey, op. cit., vol. i, pp. 168-172.

13. J. D. Lang, *Origins and Migrations of the Polynesian Nation* (Sydney, 1877), pp. vii, 4-8, 98 *et seq.*

14. W. W. Gill, *Life in the Southern Isles* (London, 1876), p. 22.

15. Pritchard, op. cit., preface and pp. 402-403.

16. D. Porter, *Journal of a Cruise made to the Pacific Ocean* (Philadelphia, 1815), vol. ii, pp. 54-55, 135-136.

17. E. Lucett, *Rovings in the Pacific* (London, 1851), vol. i, pp. 177-178.

18. G. Turner, *Samoa* (London, 1884), p. 275.

19. Burrows, op. cit., pp. 48-49.

20. R. W. Firth, *Primitive Polynesian Economy* (London, 1939), pp. 42, 48.

21. Lang, op. cit., p. 14.

22. Porter, op. cit., vol. ii, pp. 54-55.

23. A. P. Vayda, 'A Voyage by Polynesian Exiles', *Journal of the Polynesian Society*, vol. lxvii, pp. 324-329.

24. Suggs, op. cit., pp. 82-85, 106.

25. G. Vason, *An Authentic Narrative of Four Years' Residence at Tongataboo* (London, 1810), pp. 189-190.

CHAPTER FIVE: THE VOYAGING TRADITIONS

1. E. G. Burrows, 'Western Polynesia. A Study in Cultural Differentiation', *Ethnological Studies* (Gothenburg, 1938), pp. 73-76.

2. J. Banks, *The Endeavour Journal of Joseph Banks*, ed. J. C. Beaglehole (Sydney, 1962), vol. i, pp. 462-463.

3. For geographical information given to Cook and associates on first voyage by Tupaea and other Tahitians, J. Cook, *The Journals of Captain James Cook*, ed. J. C. Beaglehole, vol. i (Hakluyt Society, 1955), pp. 291-294; Forster, op. cit., pp. 511-525.

4. A. S. Thomson, *The Story of New Zealand* (London, 1859), vol. i, pp. 59-68.

5. S. P. Smith, 'The Lore of the Whare-wananga (part 2, chs. 3-5)', *Journal of the Polynesian Society*, vol. xxii, pp. 107-133, 169-218; E. Best, 'Maori and Maruiwi', *Transactions and Proceedings of the New Zealand Institute*, vol. xlviii, pp. 435-447, 'Maori Voyagers and their Vessels', ibid., vol. xlviii, pp. 447-463.

6. E. S. C. Handy, 'History and Culture in the Society Islands', *Bishop Museum Bulletin 79*, pp. 7-8; K. Luomala, 'The Menehune of Polynesia', *Bishop Museum Bulletin 203*. See also Cook, op. cit., p. 156n.

7. G. Grey, *Polynesian Mythology and Ancient Traditional History of the New Zealand Race* (London, 1855), pp. 123-181.

8. Smith's and Best's reconstructions were originally given for the most part in the sources cited under 3 above, but were later adapted by them in some respects. For a standard traditionalist reconstruction of prehistoric migrations to New Zealand, including identification of Hawaiki with Raiatea, see P. H. Buck, *The Coming of the Maori* (Wellington, 1949), pp. 4-64.

9. E. Best, 'The Astronomical Knowledge of the Maori', *Dominion Museum Monograph 3*, pp. 228-229; H. Kaamira, 'The Story of Kupe', ed. B. Biggs, *Journal of the Polynesian Society*, vol. lxvi, p. 241.

10. P. H. Buck, 'Ethnology of Mangareva', *Bishop Museum Bulletin 157*, pp. 22-23.

11. E. S. C. Handy, 'Marquesan Legends', *Bishop Museum Bulletin 69*, pp. 81-85; S. Delmas, *La religion ou le paganisme des marquisiens* (Paris, 1927), pp. 36-37.

12. A. Métraux, *Easter Island* (London, 1957), pp. 208-209.

13. Grey, op. cit., pp. 52-54, 81-89; J. C. Andersen, *Myths and Legends of the Polynesians* (London, 1928), pp. 209-245.

14. For an appropriate comment on Kupe's exploits in the Chathams, see editorial note in *Journal of the Polynesian Society*, vol. xxxiii, pp. 221-222.

15. W. Colenso, 'The Maori Races of New Zealand', *Transactions and Proceedings of the New Zealand Institute*, vol. i, essays, pp. 48, 59.

16. Banks, op. cit., vol. i, pp. 446-447.

17. S. P. Smith, *Hawaiki: the Original Home of the Maori* (Wellington, 1910), pp. 66, 68.

18. Porter, op. cit., vol. ii, pp. 54-55.

19. Grey, op. cit., p. 134.

20. Buck, op. cit., pp. 21-22.

21. Delmas, op. cit., p. 52.

22. W. W. Gill, *Myths and Songs of the South Pacific* (London, 1876), pp. 74-75, 'The Origin of the Island Manihiki', *Journal of the Polynesian Society*, vol. xxiv, pp. 145-150.

23. Cf. E. S. C. Handy, 'History and Culture in the Society Islands', *Bishop Museum Bulletin 79*, p. 15, 'Marquesan Legends', *Bishop Museum Bulletin 69*, pp. 81-85, 131.

24. A. Fornander, 'Fornander Collection of Hawaiian Antiquities and Folk-Lore', *Bishop Museum Memoirs*, vol. iv, part 1, pp. 12-13, vol. vi, no. 2, pp. 241-255.

25. Cook, op. cit., p. 156n.; Banks, op. cit., vol. i, p. 329.

26. Buck, op. cit., pp. 329-333; Smith, op. cit., pp. 262-264; Maretu, manuscript memoirs, Alexander Turnbull Library (reference to Rangiatea in Rarotonga).

27. T. Barthel, *Grundlagen zur Entzifferung der Osterinselschrift* (Hamburg, 1958), pp. 228-229.

28. T. Henry, 'Ancient Tahiti', *Bishop Museum Bulletin 48*, pp. 399-402.

29. Fornander, op. cit., vol. vi, no. 2, pp. 264-265.

30. Suggs, op. cit., p. 149.

31. Andersen, op. cit., p. 36.

32. Cf. Fornander, op. cit., vol. vi, no. 2, p. 259.

33. P. H. Buck, *Vikings of the Sunrise* (Philadelphia, 1938), p. 114.

34. Suggs, op. cit., p. 83.

35. E.g., J. L. A. de Quatrefages, *Les Polynésiens et leur migrations* (Paris, 1866); Smith, op. cit.; Suggs, op. cit., p. 149; Parsonson, op. cit., pp. 45-50.

36. J. Cook, *The Journals of Captain James Cook*, ed. J. C. Beaglehole, vol. ii (Hakluyt Society, 1961), pp. 230-426.

37. B. G. Corney (ed.), *The Quest and Occupation of Tahiti by Emissaries of Spain*, vol. ii (Hakluyt Society, 1915), pp. 293, 300.

38. S. P. Smith, *The Geographical Knowledge of the Polynesians* (paper read to Australasian Association for the Advancement of Science, Sydney, 1898), pp. 2-4.

39. A. Métraux, 'Ethnology of Easter Island', *Bishop Museum Bulletin 160*, pp. 33-34.

40. J. B. Stair, *Old Samoa* (London, 1897), pp. 271-289.

41. S. P. Smith, *Hawaiki: the Original Home of the Maori* (Wellington, 1910), pp. 272-287.

42. H. W. Williams, 'The Maruiwi Myth', *Journal of the Polynesian Society*, vol. xlvi, pp. 105-122.

43. Prout, op. cit., pp. 48-49; J. Williams, op. cit., pp. 196, 509.

44. E. G. Burrows, 'Ethnology of Uvea', *Bishop Museum Bulletin 145*, pp. 50-52.

45. Maretu, op. cit.

46. W. W. Gill, *Life in the Southern Isles* (London, 1876), pp. 22-26, 242, 249-250, 260-270.

47. E. and P. Beaglehole, 'Ethnology of Pukapuka', *Bishop Museum Bulletin 150*, pp. 400-411.

48. D. Marshall, *Ra'ivavae* (New York, 1961), pp. 33, 161, 163-164.

49. W. W. Gill, *Myths and Songs of the South Pacific* (London, 1876), pp. 142-149.

CHAPTER SIX: MIGRANTS FROM THREE KINGDOMS

1. Editorial note, *Journal of the Polynesian Society*, vol. xxx, pp. 221-223.

2. G. Turner, *Nineteen Years in Polynesia* (London, 1861), p. 192.

3. L. H. MacDaniels, 'A Study of the *fe'i* Banana and its Distribution with reference to Polynesian Migrations', *Bishop Museum Bulletin 190*, pp. 3-4, 12, 51.

4. Métraux, op. cit., pp. 13, 19, 153-154.

5. J. Williams, op. cit., p. 297.

6. Gill, op. cit., p. 135.

7. W. Bligh, *A Voyage to the South Sea* (London, 1792), p. 147.

8. Martin, op. cit., vol. i, p. 265.

9. J. Cook, *The Journals of Captain James Cook*, ed. J. C. Beaglehole, vol. i (Hakluyt Society, 1955), pp. 139-140, 159n.

10. J. Williams, op. cit., pp. 151-152.

11. E. S. C. Handy, 'The Problem of Polynesian Origins', *Bishop Museum Occasional Papers*, vol. ix, no. 8, pp. 22-23; R. Piddington, in part 2 of R. W. Williamson and R. Piddington, *Essays in Polynesian Ethnology* (Cambridge, 1939), pp. 224-225.

12. Goodenough, op. cit., pp. 148-151.

13. Suggs, op. cit., pp. 111-118.

14. E. G. Burrows, 'Western Polynesia. A Study in Cultural Differentiation', *Ethnological Studies* (Gothenburg, 1938); S. H.

Elbert, 'Internal Relationships of Polynesian Languages and Dialects', *Southwestern Journal of Anthropology*, vol. ix, pp. 147-173.

15. A. P. Vayda, 'Polynesian Cultural Distributions in New Perspective', *American Anthropologist*, vol. lxvi, pp. 817-828.
16. R. Duff, 'Neolithic Adzes of Eastern Polynesia', *Anthropology in the South Seas*, ed. J. D. Freeman and W. R. Geddes (New Plymouth, 1959), pp. 143-144.
17. Suggs, op. cit., pp. 104-105.
18. Duff, op. cit., pp. 121-127.

CHAPTER SEVEN: THE LONELY ISLANDS

1. For vegetation of mid-Pacific equatorial atolls, E. Christophersen, 'Vegetation of Pacific Equatorial Islands', *Bishop Museum Bulletin 44*. For archaeology, K. P. Emory, 'Archaeology of the Pacific Equatorial Islands', *Bishop Museum Bulletin 123*, 'Additional Notes on the Archaeology of Fanning Island', *Bishop Museum Occasional Papers*, vol. xv, no. 17; B. R. Finney, 'Recent Finds from Washington and Fanning Islands', *Journal of the Polynesian Society*, vol. lxvii, pp. 70-72.
2. Suggs, op. cit., p. 116.
3. For ethnology of these islands, P. H. Buck, 'Ethnology of Tongareva', *Bishop Museum Bulletin 92*, 'Ethnology of Manihiki and Rakahanga', *Bishop Museum Bulletin 99*; E. and P. Beaglehole, 'Ethnology of Pukapuka', *Bishop Museum Bulletin 150*; G. Macgregor, 'Ethnology of Tokelau Islands', *Bishop Museum Bulletin 146*; Vayda, op. cit.
4. Hale, op. cit., pp. 150-155, 166.
5. G. Macgregor, 'Anthropological Work of the Templeton Crocker Expedition', *Bishop Museum Annual Report for 1933*, pp. 38-43; K. P. Emory, 'Archaeology of the Phoenix Islands', *Bishop Museum Special Publication 34*; E. H. Bryan, *American Polynesia* (Honolulu, 1941), pp. 70, 73, 82.
6. H. E. Maude, 'The Colonization of the Phoenix Islands', *Journal of the Polynesian Society*, vol. lxi, pp. 62-89.
7. P. H. Buck, *Vikings of the Sunrise* (Philadelphia, 1938), pp. 59-60, 63.
8. Elbert, op. cit., pp. 159, 166.
9. Hydrographic Department, Admiralty, op. cit., vol. iii, p. 43.
10. E. N. Ferdon, 'Comparisons', in 'Archaeology of Easter Island,

K

vol. i', *Monographs of the School of American Research and the Museum of New Mexico 24*, part 1, pp. 533-535.

11. T. Heyerdahl, *Aku-Aku* (London, 1958), p. 127.

12. Métraux, op. cit., p. 417.

13. H. Lavachery, 'Contributions a l'étude de l'archaeologie de l'île Pitcairn', *Société des américanistes de Belgique Bulletin 19*; Buck, op. cit., pp. 216-221.

14. H. Laval, *Mangareva* (Braine-le-Comte, 1938), p. 15n.

15. Duff, op. cit., figure 9, p. 142.

16. Heyerdahl, op. cit., pp. 323-345.

17. J. A. Moerenhout, *Voyages aux îles du grand océan* (Paris, 1837), vol. ii, pp. 331-332.

18. Morrison, op. cit., p. 68.

19. Cook, op. cit., pp. 291-294; Forster, op. cit., pp. 521-522.

20. J. Williams, op. cit., pp. 38-40.

21. Ellis, op. cit., vol. iii, p. 90.

22. Moerenhout, op. cit., vol. i, p. 152, vol. ii, pp. 346-348.

23. J. Williams, op. cit., pp. 86-88.

24. W. W. Gill, *Life in the Southern Isles* (London, 1876), pp. 15, 102-103.

25. Bligh, op. cit., p. 147.

26. J. Williams, op. cit., p. 68.

27. Corney, op. cit., vol. ii, p. 300.

28. J. Cook, *A Voyage to the Pacific Ocean* (London, 1784), vol. ii, pp. 177-178.

29. Elbert, op. cit., pp. 63-164; Burrows, op. cit., p. 192.

30. Cook, op. cit., vol. i, pp. 368-369.

31. S. P. Smith, note 28, *Journal of the Polynesian Society*, vol. ii, p. 126.

32. Buck, op. cit., pp. 44-45.

33. C. Markham, *The Voyages of Pedro Fernandez de Quiros 1595 to 1606* (Hakluyt Society, 1904), vol. ii, pp. 493-494.

34. R. W. Firth, 'Anuta and Tikopia: symbiotic elements in social organisation', *Journal of the Polynesian Society*, vol. lxiii, pp. 89-92.

35. R. H. Codrington, *The Melanesians* (Oxford, 1891), p. 6.

36. Dillon, op. cit., vol. ii, p. 138.

37. Elbert, op. cit., p. 148.

38. Hornell, op. cit., pp. 395-398.

39. Kotzebue, op. cit., vol. iii, pp. 98, 126, 193.

CHAPTER EIGHT: EARLY MAN IN NEW ZEALAND

1. For linguistic affinities, Elbert, op. cit.; for cultural affinities, see summary of research in J. Golson, 'Culture Change in Prehistoric New Zealand', *Anthropology in the South Seas*, eds. J. R. Freeman and W. R. Geddes (New Plymouth, 1959), pp. 36-37, 47-48.

2. National Geographic Society, op. cit.

3. New Zealand Press Association report, 9 September 1953; *Evening Post*, Wellington, 7 March 1957.

4. *Evening Post*, Wellington, 30 November 1957.

5. Golson, op. cit., pp. 36-47; H. S. Jansen, 'Comparison between Ring-dates and 14C-dates in a New Zealand Kauri Tree', *New Zealand Journal of Science*, vol. v, pp. 74-84.

6. Grey, op. cit., pp. 143-161; P. H. Buck, *The Coming of the Maori* (Wellington, 1949), pp. 4-64.

7. J. W. Stack, 'Sketch of the Traditional History of the South Island Maoris', *Transactions and Proceedings of the New Zealand Institute*, vol. x, p. 61

8. H. Stowell, 'Maori Migrations', *New Zealand Herald*, 20 June-18 July 1925; 'The Ancient Maori. III. Canoe Migrations', *Christchurch Weekly Press*, 7 October 1926.

9. E. Shortland, *The Southern Districts of New Zealand* (London, 1851), p. 102.

10. H. D. Skinner, 'The Morioris of the Chatham Islands', *Bishop Museum Memoir 9*, no. 1; H. D. Skinner and W. J. Phillipps, 'Necklaces, Pendants and Amulets from the Chatham Islands and New Zealand', *Journal of the Polynesian Society*, vol. lxii, pp. 169-183; R. Duff, *The Moa-hunter Period of Maori Culture* (Wellington, 1950), pp. 7, 31.

11. Prout, op. cit., p. 48.

12. Duff, op. cit., p. 31.

13. Ibid., pp. 163-167.

14. Banks, op. cit., vol. i, pp. 455-456.

CHAPTER NINE: THE POLYNESIAN MIGRATION TRAIL

1. For summary and critique of sunken land theories of Dumont d'Urville, Moerenhout, and others, see A. Lesson, *Les Polynésiens*, vol. i, pp. 386-428.

2. E.g., K. B. Cumberland, 'The Pacific Islands and its Ocean Groups', *Post-Primary School Bulletin* (New Zealand), vol. iii, no. 5, pp. 100-102.

3. J. M. de Zuñiga, *An Historical View of the Philippine Islands* (London, 1814), vol. i, p. 33; W. Ellis, *Narrative of a Tour through Hawaii* (London, 1827), p. 442, *Polynesian Researches* (London, 1831), vol. i, pp. 125-127; T. Heyerdahl, *American Indians in the Pacific* (London, 1952), *Aku-Aku* (London, 1958), pp. 350-359.

4. E.g., A. Lesson, op. cit., vol. i, pp. 429-516; R. Heine-Geldern, 'Some Problems of Migration in the Pacific', *Kultur und Sprache*, ed. W. Koppers, *Beiträge zur Kulturgeschichte und Linguistik*, IX, pp. 313-362.

5. E.g., for Melanesian provenance, Gill, op. cit., pp. 22-26, 242, 249-250, 260-270; Hale, op. cit., pp. 174-186; S. P. Smith, 'The Polynesian Sojourn in Fiji', *Journal of the Polynesian Society*, vol. iii, pp. 145-152; G. W. Grace, 'Austronesian Linguistics and Culture History', *American Anthropologist*, vol. lxiii, pp. 359-368; and for Micronesian route, Buck, op. cit., pp. 41-45, 58-63; H. D. Skinner, 'Some Aspects of the History of Polynesian Material Culture', *Journal of the Polynesian Society*, vol. i, pp. 42-43.

6. E.g., Buck, op. cit., pp. 64-283.

7. T. Heyerdahl and A. Skjölsvold, 'Archaeological Evidence of Pre-Spanish Visits to the Galapagos Islands', *Society of American Archaeology Memoir 12*; T. Heyerdahl, *Aku-Aku* (London, 1958), pp. 13, 354-356.

8. Reports of paper by Heyerdahl at Tenth Pacific Science Congress in *Dominion*, Wellington, 24 August 1961, and report by D. S. Milne in 'Time-Erased Wake of Pacific Migrations', *Evening Post*, Wellington, 8 September 1961.

9. R. T. Simmons and J. J. Graydon, 'A Blood Group Genetical Survey in Eastern and Central Polynesians', *American Journal of Physical Anthropology*, vol. xv, pp. 357-366.

10. R. T. Simmons, 'Blood Group Genes in Polynesians and Comparisons with other Pacific Peoples', *Oceania*, vol. xxxii, pp. 198-210.

11. E. Goldschmidt, 'An Interpretation of Polynesian Blood-Group Gene Frequencies', in Pacific Science Association, *Abstracts of Symposium Papers, Tenth Pacific Science Congress*, p. 99.

12. W. C. Boyd, *Genetics and the Races of Man* (Boston, 1950).

13. T. F. Cheeseman, *Manual of the New Zealand Flora* (Wellington, 1925), p. 262.

14. H. D. Skinner, 'Some Recent Publications relating to Easter Island Culture and its Probable History', *Journal of the Polynesian Society*, vol. lxvii, p. 250.

15. E. D. Merrill, 'The Botany of Cook's Voyages', *Chronica Botanica*, vol. xiv, pp. 171, 321.

16. D. E. Yen, 'The Sweet Potato in the Pacific: The Propagation of the Plant in relation to its Distribution', *Journal of the Polynesian Society*, vol. lxix, pp. 368-375.

17. B. Seemann, *The Botany of the Voyage of H.M.S. "Herald"* (London, 1852-7), p. 319.

18. A. Sharp, 'Ancient Voyagers in the Pacific', *Polynesian Society Memoir 32*, pp. 61-63.

19. For summary of botanical evidence, Heine-Geldern, op. cit., pp. 343-355.

20. J. Hornell, 'Was there Pre-Columbian Contact between the Peoples of Oceania and America?', *Journal of the Polynesian Society*, vol. liv, p. 183.

21. For summaries of expert opinion, G. W. Grace, 'The Position of the Polynesian Languages within the Austronesian (Malayo-Polynesian) Language Family', *International Journal of American Linguistics Memoir 16*, pp. 3-9; A. Capell, 'Oceanic Linguistics Today', and sundry commentators, *Current Anthropology*, vol. iii, pp. 371-428.

22. Gill, op. cit., pp. 22-26, 242, 249-250, 260-270; Hale, op. cit., pp. 174-186; Smith, op. cit.

23. Grace, op. cit.

24. I. Dyen, 'The Lexicostatistical Classification of the Malayo-polynesian Languages', *Language*, vol. xxxviii, pp. 38-46.

25. Suggs, op. cit., pp. 68-72, 87-93, 111-116; J. Golson, 'Polynesian Culture History,' review article on Suggs, op. cit., *Journal of the Polynesian Society*, vol. lxx, pp. 498-508.

26. E.g., Buck, op. cit., pp. 41-45, 58-63, 307-312; H. D. Skinner, 'Some Aspects of the History of Polynesian Material Culture', *Journal of the Polynesian Society*, vol. 1, pp. 42-43.

27. Gill, op. cit., pp. 22-26, 242, 249-250, 260-270.

28. Markham, op. cit., vol. i, pp. 51, 142-143, 227.

29. I. Lee, *Captain Bligh's Second Voyage to the South Sea* (London, 1920), pp. 153-155.

30. Buck, op. cit., pp. 48-49.
31. R. P. Lesson *et al.*, 'Zoologie', vol. i, part 1, in L. I. Duperrey *et al.*, *Voyage autour du monde* (Paris, 1826-30), p. 72.
32. Buck, op. cit., pp. 47-48.
33. Cook, op. cit., vol. i, p. 374.
34. G. Brown, *Melanesians and Polynesians* (London, 1910), p. 436.
35. Hilder, op. cit., pp. 91-92, table II, p. 148.
36. Burrows, op. cit., pp. 73-76.
37. Elbert, op. cit., pp. 159, 165-166.
38. Suggs, op. cit., pp. 109-130.
39. Ibid., pp. 88-89; Golson, op. cit., p. 500.
40. Dillon, op. cit., vol. ii, p. 104.
41. Kotzebue, op. cit., vol. ii, pp. 122-123.
42. National Geographic Society, op. cit.
43. Elbert, op. cit.
44. Delmas, op. cit., p. 52; P. H. Buck, 'Ethnology of Mangareva', *Bishop Museum Bulletin 157*, p. 100.
45. Duff, op. cit., pp. 12, 228-233; cf. Sharp, op. cit., pp. 103-104.
46. K. P. Emory, W. J. Bonk, and Y. H. Sinoto, 'Hawaiian Archaeology: Fishhooks', *Bishop Museum Special Publication 47*; 'Society Islands Archaeological Discovery', *News from Bishop Museum*, August 1962.
47. Ibid.

INDEX